W9-BAS-864

5 1230 00971 0241

The Urbana Free Library

To renew: call **217-367-4057**
or go to **urbanafreelibrary.org**
and select **My Account**

DISCARDED BY THE
URBANA FREE LIBRARY

THE UNABOMBER

FBI FILES

THE UNABOMBER

Agent Kathy Puckett and the Hunt for a Serial Bomber

BRYAN DENSON

ROARING BROOK PRESS

NEW YORK

Copyright © 2019 by Bryan Denson

Published by Roaring Brook Press
Roaring Brook Press is a division of Holtzbrinck Publishing Holdings
Limited Partnership
175 Fifth Avenue, New York, NY 10010

mackids.com

All rights reserved

Library of Congress Control Number: 2018955824

ISBN 978-1-250-19913-3

Our books may be purchased in bulk for promotional, educational, or
business use. Please contact your local bookseller or the Macmillan
Corporate and Premium Sales Department at (800) 221-7945 ext. 5442 or
by email at MacmillanSpecialMarkets@macmillan.com.

First edition, 2019
Book design by Aram Kim
Printed in the United States of America by LSC Communications,
Harrisonburg, Virginia

1   3   5   7   9   10   8   6   4   2

In memory of my mother, Patricia Jean Denson,
one of the great moms from the greatest generation

KEY CHARACTERS

UNABOM Task Force

Jim R. Freeman, special agent in charge of the FBI's San Francisco Field Office

Terry D. Turchie, assistant special agent in charge of the UNABOM Task Force (UTF)

Donald Max Noel, supervisory special agent

James "Fitz" Fitzgerald, supervisory special agent

Joel Moss, supervisory special agent

Kathleen M. Puckett, special agent

Lee Stark, special agent

Washington, D.C., Characters

U.S. Attorney General Janet Reno

FBI Director Louis J. Freeh

Molly Flynn, special agent in the FBI's Washington Metropolitan Field Office

Kaczynski Family

Theodore J. "Ted" Kaczynski, suspect no. 2,416

David Kaczynski, Ted's younger brother

Linda Patrik, David's wife

Wanda Kaczynski, Ted and David's mother

Anthony "Tony" Bisceglie, David Kaczynski and Linda Patrik's lawyer

Montana Characters

Tom McDaniel, FBI senior resident agent

Jerry Burns, U.S. Forest Service law enforcement officer

Bernie Hubley, assistant U.S. attorney

Clifford "Butch" Gehring Jr., Kaczynski's neighbor in Lincoln, Montana

PROLOGUE

FBI badge.

Take a close look at the badge on this page.

The shield is gold plated, stands two and a half inches tall, and comes with a solemn pledge. The FBI agents who carry these badges promise to defend the Constitution. They promise to protect Americans from all enemies. They promise to protect us no matter who our attackers might be, and where they might strike.

Fourteen thousand special agents of the Federal Bureau of Investigation, backed by 21,000 support personnel, carry those badges. They work night and day in every state, territory, and corner of the world. They live by the FBI motto "Fidelity, Bravery, Integrity."

In the early days of the organization, America's worst threats were at home. In the 1930s, gun-toting gangsters with names like Al "Scarface" Capone, Charles "Pretty Boy" Floyd, and George "Machine Gun Kelly" Barnes got rich robbing banks, kidnapping children for ransom, and operating illegal bars and casinos. The FBI declared war on these "public enemies," and succeeded in taking many off the streets. But in the last half of the twentieth century, Americans faced new and greater dangers in the homeland.

Highly organized street gangs, the Mafia, outlaw bikers, and domestic terrorists became targets of the bureau. The most dangerous were white-supremacist groups such as the Ku Klux Klan. From the civil rights era into the 1980s, those secretive groups terrorized and sometimes killed people of color with fists, firearms, and explosives—and still do even today. By the late 1990s, the FBI declared America's leading domestic terrorist threat to be underground groups such as the Earth Liberation Front, which firebombed businesses and government agencies it accused of harming the natural world.

Then, in a single morning, the FBI's mission changed forever.

On September 11, 2001, al Qaeda terrorists boarded

four jetliners on the East Coast. Once in the air, they seized control of the planes. In eighty-one minutes, they flew them into the World Trade Center towers in New York, the Pentagon in Virginia, and, thanks to intervening passengers, a field in Pennsylvania. Those men, on a suicide mission, murdered nearly three thousand innocent people. It was the deadliest terrorist attack in U.S. history—a foreign attack on the American homeland.

The attacks of 9/11 changed the FBI overnight. Agents still catch bank robbers, kidnappers, and other criminals, but their primary mission today is to protect Americans from terrorists, spies, organized crime, public corruption, cyberattacks, and assaults on our economic, military, and political systems.

Books in the FBI Files series spotlight the FBI's most amazing cases since the bureau began on July 26, 1908. You will meet some of America's worst villains and the heroic men and women who brought them to justice. And you will understand why FBI agents live by the motto "Fidelity, Bravery, Integrity."

CHAPTER I

On the afternoon of April 24, 1995, a sunny
Monday, a strange package arrived at the California Forestry Association's headquarters in Sacramento. It was
the size of a shoebox, wrapped in plain brown paper,
and heavy. Workers gathered around the parcel, which
sat on a desk, and looked it over. A scientist who worked
in the office lifted the box, gave it a shake.

"It's heavy enough to be a bomb," he joked.

Gilbert Murray, the association's president, chuckled
along with his co-worker. Murray was a handsome,
balding man with a boyish smile. Friends called him Gil.
His organization promoted the timber industry, which
cut down trees to build things like houses and furniture.
Many environmentalists cursed loggers for cutting down

too many trees, sometimes turning forestland into stumps. But Murray could scarcely imagine any of them being so angry that they would mail a bomb to his office. Still, when a pregnant co-worker began to cut into the paper with scissors, Murray stopped her.

"Let me do that for you," he said.

Murray carried the package to his office and placed it on the desk. It was addressed to William Dennison, the association's former president. Murray figured the contents of the parcel were intended for his organization, not Dennison, who had retired a year earlier. He stood hunched over the package and began to cut through the strong tape. His work revealed a wooden box, which he began to open.

It would be the last thing he ever saw.

A deafening explosion shook the office, a blast so powerful it shattered windows and shot pieces of furniture sixty feet across the office. Two doors in the office hurtled off their hinges. The noise sent workers racing out of the building. They gathered outside, ears still ringing, as black smoke poured from the one-story brick building. They smelled chemicals. Murray's panicked co-workers knew he was still in the building.

"Gil!" one woman shrieked. "Gil!"

No response.

By lifting the box's lid, Murray had triggered a bomb tucked neatly inside.

Dick Ross, special agent in charge of the FBI's Sacramento office, raced to the California Forestry Association and stalked into Murray's office before police could close down the crime scene with yellow tape. Ross's eyes roved from Murray's corpse, which lay on the floor, to fragments of bomb parts and pooled and splattered blood. He was looking for clues. Ross saw in the wreckage the work of a mysterious bomber who had terrorized America for nearly seventeen years.

The culprit had now mailed or secretly hand delivered sixteen bombs from 1978 until that spring day in 1995. Fourteen had exploded, leaving three people dead and twenty-three injured. Most of the bomber's targets had connections to universities or airlines. The FBI code-named its case UNABOM, short for UNiversity, Airline, BOMbing. Agents on the UNABOM Task Force, along with news reporters and the public, called the mysterious killer the "Unabomber."

Ross was shaken by the scene inside the California Forestry Association building, just ten blocks from his own office. Yet he was all business when he phoned the

FBI's San Francisco Field Office. He reached Terry D. Turchie, who supervised the team.

"Terry," he said. "We've had a bombing up here. Everything about it looks like UNABOM. I've closed down the scene."

The first agent out the door was Pat Webb, a bomb expert. He hopped into the driver's seat of his brand-new FBI car, flipped on its flashing emergency lights, and gunned the engine. Webb reached Sacramento, more than eighty miles northeast of his San Francisco office, in record time. At 5:30 that evening, he entered the crime scene, where Gil Murray's body remained on the floor. Webb observed brown paper glued to pieces of the wooden box, batteries stripped of wrappers and covered in tape, and other familiar bomb parts. All were Unabomber trademarks.

Webb walked outside and took a seat on the curb. He phoned Turchie in San Francisco and delivered the cold facts: "Terry, this is a UNABOM event." But it was more than that. The Unabomber's newest explosive was more powerful than any of his previous bombs.

The UNABOM Task Force spent days bagging and tagging bomb parts and other evidence. Agents shipped them to the FBI Laboratory in Quantico, Virginia. They hoped the bureau's forensic analysts could find a fiber or a fingerprint—anything they could link to the bomber.

Agents also hoped the killer would claim responsibility for the latest crime. He had grown bolder in his recent attacks, mailing letters to newspapers in which he bragged about his bombings and taunted the FBI. He identified himself as a terrorist group called "FC."

On the very day Murray died, *The New York Times* received a long, typewritten letter. "The FBI has tried to portray these bombings as the work of an isolated nut," the Unabomber wrote. "We won't waste our time arguing about whether we are nuts. . . . Clearly we are in a position to do a great deal of damage. And it doesn't appear that the FBI is going to catch us any time soon. The FBI is a joke."

CHAPTER 2

Special Agent Kathleen M. Puckett was sickened by the latest mail-bomb murder. Puckett, whose FBI colleagues called her Kathy, had joined the UNABOM Task Force the previous fall. During her first few months in the assignment, the bomber killed twice. The first of those bombings, in December 1994, killed an advertising executive in the kitchen of his New Jersey home. Then came the bomb that took Murray's life.

Puckett and other members of the task force were certain they could catch the killer.

"The case was solvable," Puckett recalled years later, "because the killer was a human being." She knew Turchie, her boss, felt the same way. He was the soul of the investigation, cheering on agents wearied by long hours on the job. Puckett and Turchie felt uncommonly driven to catch the killer, who seemed equally driven to keep killing.

Turchie and Puckett had known each other for years. They had worked together to prevent spies for the Soviet Union, America's biggest enemy, from stealing U.S. secrets. Turchie had been impressed by Puckett's instincts and creative thinking. He had recruited her onto the UNABOM Task Force in hopes she could draw up a behavioral profile of the killer. He knew that getting inside the bomber's mind might pave the way to catching him.

Puckett's best evidence was in the letters the killer had mailed to newspapers, professors, and even one of his victims without betraying his real identity. Puckett pored over those letters. Each word offered a potential clue about the bomber. She came to believe that "FC" was most likely just one person—someone smart, highly educated, and working alone. She also believed it was a man, because all of America's most notorious bombers had been males.

The FBI Laboratory, which studied the evidence from the bomb site, came back with bad news for the investigators: The killer had left no physical evidence. Not a fingerprint. Not even a trace of sweat. Now it was up to Puckett to study the bomber's latest note to *The New York Times*. Catching the killer without knowing who wrote the letter would be a monumental feat. Still, she believed his words could help her shape a behavioral profile that might help to identify him.

What she couldn't possibly know was the unique role she would play in unmasking the Unabomber.

Nothing in Puckett's early life suggested a career in the FBI. She was born in 1950, a time when women were not even allowed to serve as agents. She went to high school and college in Southern California during the 1960s. It was a place and time in which people her age were protesting the Vietnam War and mocking the U.S. government—including the FBI—and young Kathy Puckett had been one of them. She studied history and anthropology—subjects not likely to impress FBI recruiters.

Puckett traveled across Europe after college and joined the air force in 1973. The military was a smart career choice for women back then—one of only a few jobs that paid men and women equally. She was recruited into the Office of Special Investigations, which protects the U.S. military from spies and terrorists. The

Air Force sent her to Seattle, Washington, where she worked in counterintelligence, a field that prevents spying by foreign enemies. Her most important duty was preventing Soviet spies from stealing secrets from U.S. Navy submarine bases. Puckett's hard work helped earn her a promotion to captain.

Her talent caught the attention of the FBI and the Central Intelligence Agency (better known as the CIA), both of which tried to recruit her. She had worked with FBI agents during her air force years, but the bureau was a no-frills organization. FBI recruiters didn't wine and dine her. They just told her where the entrance exam would be given and what time to be there. CIA recruiters took a different approach. They flew her around the country, bought her nice meals. They offered her the chance to go to Greece as a covert operator—a real, live American spy. While Puckett was thrilled to be courted by the agency, choosing to become a professional spy was a major decision. She would not be allowed to tell people what she did for a living. This meant she would have to lie to the people she loved most—even her parents.

The CIA *and* FBI offered Puckett jobs. She made her choice in the middle of 1978, and reported for training at the FBI Academy. In a remarkable coincidence, Puckett

Puckett was working as a spy hunter on Counterintelligence Squad 12 on the sixth floor of the Federal Building in San Francisco when this photo was taken in about 1990. The photo behind her was of the Soviet Union's consulate, a den of spies targeted by the FBI.

entered duty with the FBI on May 21, 1978, just five days before the Unabomber's first bomb went off.

Puckett slogged through hard physical training at the FBI Academy, which sits on a sprawling Marine Corps base in Quantico, Virginia. She was a tall Californian—a shade under five foot ten—with suntanned cheeks and a head full of long blond hair. But she was not a natural athlete; Puckett forced herself to run on hot, muggy days in spite of painful shin splints. She sailed right through her classroom work, mostly legal training, and surprised herself by scoring high marks at the firing range. She found it satisfying to beat burly SWAT team members at skeet shooting. Puckett and another woman in her class were among the first 130 women ever allowed to serve as FBI agents.

Once she got into decent shape, one of the men in her class pulled her aside. "Well," he said, "if we have to have women agents, Kathy, I think that you're the kind we need." His comment was supposed to be a compliment, but it wasn't. Puckett didn't want to be respected as a *female* agent. She wanted respect as an agent.

Her day would come.

CHAPTER 3

Kathy Puckett's 1994 entrance onto the UNABOM investigation, which had been going on for about fifteen years, made her a newcomer to the case. So it was clear to her that she had to bone up on the bombings. It was important to walk where the bomber had walked, see what he'd seen. Soon she got the chance.

Puckett's time on the task force began with what might be called a creepy field trip. She and other agents traveled to Chicago to look at the scene of the Unabomber's first attack. Puckett found herself transported to a time when the president was Jimmy Carter, NASA announced its first women astronauts, and the first Star Wars movie was still a hit.

On the trip, Puckett learned that the Unabomber's

first bomb had been a mistake. He had attempted to mail his package in Chicago in May 1978. But he discovered that it was too big to fit through the slot of a mailbox, so he left it in a parking lot. A woman who found the package saw that the sender was listed as Northwestern University Professor Buckley Crist Jr., so she arranged to get it to him.

Crist took one look at the package and knew something was wrong. Someone had written his name as the sender—and it wasn't him. The professor summoned a campus security officer, who opened the package. Suddenly an explosion rocked the room, leaving the officer dazed, his ears ringing. He survived the bombing, and the professor was unhurt.

Puckett analyzed that bombing from all angles. The bomber had come and gone from Chicago with ease. He'd left a package on the ground and gotten away unnoticed. Puckett told her colleagues on the UNABOM Task Force that she believed the bomber had once lived in Chicago. In time, they would learn she was right.

A year after the first bombing, a graduate student at Northwestern opened a package that held a cigar box wrapped in red polka-dot paper, detonating a bomb that left him bloody and burned. While the first two explosives were certainly traumatizing to the people who opened them, the bombs themselves had been minor, no more powerful than large firecrackers. Agents of the U.S. Bureau of Alcohol, Tobacco, and Firearms (called the Bureau of Alcohol, Tobacco, Firearms, and Explosives since 2003) investigated both bombings, but they could identify no suspects.

Then the Unabomber struck again, this time on a much larger scale.

On the cool, gray morning of November 15, 1979, American Airlines Flight 444 from Chicago's O'Hare International Airport had begun its ascent toward Washington, D.C., when the Boeing 727 jetliner suddenly shook violently. Passengers later felt intense heat beneath their feet. Then, as the crew prepared to land, black smoke poured out of the air-conditioning vents, fogging the pilots' instrument panel and filling the main cabin. Oxygen masks dropped in front of the seventy-eight people aboard. Pilots made an emergency landing at Dulles International Airport, where rescuers treated twelve people for smoke inhalation.

A fire in the cargo hold of the aircraft had caused the heat and smoke. Had that blaze grown and reached the jetliner's fuel lines, the aircraft would have become a flying inferno. Everyone on board would have died.

The FBI, which investigates attacks on American aircraft, sent bomb experts to pick through the charred cargo hold of Flight 444. They found remnants of a mail bomb built into a cottonwood box. They also found a one-dollar Eugene O'Neill stamp on the package—identical to those used in the first Unabomber attack. The bomb loaded onto Flight 444 had been equipped with a makeshift device, fashioned from a barometer, which sensed how high the plane climbed or dropped. The bomber rigged the device so it would set off the explosive when the aircraft climbed to two thousand feet.

The bomb's explosive ingredients included powders removed from rifle cartridges. The builder of the device used tape, nails, screws, and solder. Agents would look for such parts—known as a bomb maker's "signature"—in future attacks.

In early June 1980, United Airlines President Percy A. Wood received a package covered in brown paper at his stately home in Lake Forest, Illinois. Inside he found a copy of the book *Ice Brothers*. When he opened it, he heard an ear-piercing blast and felt his skin searing as if he had fallen into a fire. A pipe bomb tucked into the hollowed-out pages of the novel left Wood with cuts and burns over most of his face and body.

Federal agents collected remnants of the Unabomber's attacks, including the packaging of the bomb mailed to Percy A. Wood, the president of American Airlines. Wood survived the attack.

The Wood bombing marked the fourth mysterious explosion in just two years. FBI forensic experts examined bomb parts from both Northwestern University explosions, the Flight 444 fire, and Percy Wood's home. They decided one person was probably behind all four. So the FBI's Chicago office took over the investigation as a serial bombing case. Agents interviewed victims of all the attacks to see if they had any mutual enemies. They found no connections between them. But they did find one curious piece of evidence. After agents carefully collected pieces of the bomb parts from Wood's home, they found a small metal tag stamped with the letters

"FC." Agents had no clue what the letters stood for. Not yet.

As Puckett and her fellow agents studied those years-old case files and traveled to scenes of the UNABOM attacks, one thing became clear: The bomber had changed, and so had his explosives. He and his bombs had grown ever more dangerous.

The Unabomber struck six more times from 1981 to 1985. Explosions burned a secretary at Vanderbilt University and a professor at the University of California, Berkeley. Later, a graduate student at Berkeley picked up a beige plastic box, triggering a blast that blew four fingers off his hand, shot his college ring into a wall, and dashed his dreams of becoming an astronaut. Another explosion burned the belly, forearms, and legs of a University of Michigan student. Two other bombs—one left at the University of Utah, another mailed to a Boeing aviation plant in Auburn, Washington—failed to go off. Agents seized those unexploded bombs and blew them up at a safe distance. So far, no one had been killed.

The FBI found more clues in each of those new bombings. Whoever built the explosives had used old scraps of wood, wire, and metal. One FBI bomb expert nicknamed their culprit the "Junkyard Bomber." They

Federal agents found pieces of metal mysteriously stamped "FC" in the wreckage of many of the Unabomber's attacks.

also found a mailing label typed out with an old Smith Corona typewriter. But the FBI's scariest discovery came when agents looked at the explosive charges loaded into the latest bombs. Their bomber now used two chemicals—ammonium nitrate and aluminum powder—to create much more powerful blasts.

Their bomber had grown bolder, Puckett later explained, because *he* now felt more powerful. He could walk onto university campuses and leave explosives. He was blending in, raising no suspicions. He was a ghost. An angry ghost. And he called himself "FC."

After her field trip to the scenes of the Unabomber's old crimes, Puckett believed the culprit had a high IQ and might be a professor. She learned that the Unabomber had paid close attention to every detail of his bomb making. He carved wood by hand, wrapped parts with tape, removed serial numbers from batteries.

When Puckett and her colleagues had finished their review of the bomber's attacks, she concluded that he would never stop bombing until the FBI caught him. Until then, he would continue to perfect his bombs.

Puckett believed he had always meant to kill.

CHAPTER 4

Two weeks before Christmas 1985, nearly a decade before Puckett began to study the bomber's psychology, a handsome man named Hugh Scrutton walked out of his business into a cold, windy Wednesday afternoon in Sacramento. He was thirty-eight years old and the owner of RenTech Computer Rentals.

He walked into the first row of cars in the parking lot, heading to lunch, and spied what appeared to be a road hazard in front of his car. It was a homemade box, fashioned from two pieces of lumber, with shiny nails poking out. Scrutton bent over to move the device. By picking it up, he triggered a massive explosion from the bomb inside. Metal fragments opened a gaping hole in his chest and pierced his heart.

"Oh my God!" he shouted. "Help me!"

First responders raced to the scene and loaded Scrutton into an ambulance, but he bled to death in minutes. FBI agents swarmed the parking lot looking for clues. There they found a piece of metal with familiar letters: "FC." The Unabomber had struck again.

Scrutton was his first kill.

When the FBI confronts major crimes such as Scrutton's murder, the bureau sends a wave of agents to help. If a child turns up missing, for instance, within an hour the FBI can dispatch a hundred agents to knock on doors and search neighborhoods. The bureau's analysts—the men and women who collect, analyze, and catalog clues and other data—can quickly put together a file with every known fact about a case.

Agents fanned out across Sacramento to hunt for Scrutton's killer. They questioned more than a thousand RenTech customers and the owners of nearly a hundred cars parked at the mall. Agents also gathered the names of more than three thousand people staying in nearby hotels. An FBI database checked those names against potential UNABOM suspects. But their hard work got them nowhere. Frustrated agents hoped for some good luck.

But a year would pass before they got it.

On February 20, 1987, Tammy Fluehe looked up from her work in a Salt Lake City, Utah, computer store. A man wearing a hoodie and aviator sunglasses walked across the parking lot just outside her window. He reached into a white canvas bag, calmly pulled out a pair of boards with shiny nails sticking out one side, and placed them in front of her car tires.

"Hey!" she yelled.

The man looked at her coolly and sauntered away. Fluehe started for the door to confront him. But the owner of the store stopped her, fearing for her safety.

Later that day, the storeowner's oldest son spotted the strange object and knelt to pick it up. When he moved it, an explosion of wood and metal shot into his nose, eyes, and skull, hurling him twenty feet across the parking lot. Bomb fragments riddled his body and severed a nerve in his wrist. Miraculously, he survived.

The bomb he had picked up was a replica of the one that had killed Hugh Scrutton. And agents discovered something else in the parking lot crime scene—another

Artist Robert Exter created the first composite sketch of the Unabomber after interviewing Tammy Fluehe, who viewed the bomber from a distance of four feet.

piece of metal stamped "FC."

Fluehe was the first known eyewitness of a Unabomber attack. She later described the man she had seen to a police sketch artist, who produced a drawing. The FBI turned that image into a wanted poster. The haunting face of the hoodie-wearing bomber went global, searing itself into the minds of a frightened nation.

But the image didn't lead the FBI to the killer, and the case went cold. Weeks passed into months, and months passed into years with no new bombs. When serial lawbreakers vanish like that, it's common for investigators to assume they died or went to prison for an unrelated crime. But Kathy Puckett wasn't so sure. As she studied each of the Unabomber attacks, she was convinced that the wide circulation of the wanted poster had driven him underground. He was cagey. Puckett could see he worked more like a spy than a standard criminal.

"The more I learned," she said, "I was convinced that the reason he'd eluded law enforcement for so many years was because he was one of the most careful criminal opponents we had ever had."

Six years after the sighting by Tammy Fluehe, Dr. Charles Epstein, a brilliant scientist and concert cellist who worked at the University of California, San Francisco, opened a large envelope at his kitchen table. He heard a hissing sound and witnessed a blinding flash. The explosion blew out windows, shot pieces of wood across the house, and took three of his fingers. He survived, but it would take surgery and painful rehabilitation before he could play the cello again.

Two days later, Yale University Professor David Gelernter opened a similar package. Inside was a redwood box. When he lifted the lid, he felt the heat of an explosion. Gelernter staggered to a phone and began to dial for help, but the blast had blown off much of his right hand. Gelernter stumbled downstairs and ran to the school's infirmary. He, too, survived.

The bomber was back.

CHAPTER 5

In June 1993, an editor at *The New York Times* phoned the FBI to report that the newspaper had received a strange letter. It was mailed to the *Times* just before the Unabomber's attacks on Professors Epstein and Gelernter.

"We are an anarchist group calling ourselves FC," it read. "Notice that the postmark on this envelope precedes a newsworthy event that will happen about the time you receive this letter, if nothing goes wrong. This will prove that we knew about the event in advance, so our claim of responsibility is truthful. Ask the FBI about FC. They have heard of us. We will give information about our goals at some future time."

The note closed with a series of numbers: 553-25-4394.

We are an anarchist group calling ourselves FC. Notice that the postmark on this envelope precedes a newsworthy event that will happen about the time you receive this letter, if nothing goes wrong. This will prove that we knew about the event in advance, so our claim of responsibility is truthful. Ask the FBI about FC. They have heard of us. We will give information about our goals at some future time. Right now we only want to establish our identity and provide an identifying number that will ensure the authenticity of any future communications from us. Keep this number secret so that no one else can pretend to speak in our name.

553-25-4394

The Unabomber wrote this note to The New York Times in advance of the bombings that seriously wounded professors at Yale University and the University of California, San Francisco.

This was an authentication code known only by the bomber and the FBI. The bomber added this code to notes in which he took credit for his attacks. This unique number let the FBI know that the Unabomber sent the bomb, not a copycat.

Both the Unabomber and the FBI asked *The New York Times* not to print the code in its stories about the bombings. That way the bomber and his pursuers would always know when his letters were real. Newspapers work to tell readers what they don't know, and they typically don't like to hide information. But editors at the *Times* honored the FBI's request. They knew that printing the code might harm the FBI's investigation, so they left it out of their stories on the Unabomber.

The Unabomber got what he wanted. He had bragged about his crimes to the world using the puzzling initials FC. But the FBI also got something. The bomber had just given investigators a new sample of his writing.

Agents didn't believe the letter came from a terrorist group called FC. They were almost certain it was the work of a lone-wolf terrorist, the hardest kind to catch. It's much easier to track down a group of terrorists, because it only takes one person to make a mistake that gets everyone caught. Lone wolves plan their attacks, control the times and places of their bombings, and keep all their secrets to themselves.

Experts at the FBI Laboratory carefully examined the Unabomber's letter to the *Times* since it was their best piece of evidence. When they looked at it under a special light, they made a startling find. Someone, perhaps the bomber himself, had written a note on a separate piece of paper laid atop the letter. By pressing down with a pencil or pen, the writer had left indentations in the paper of the letter mailed to *The New York Times*. It read, "Call Nathan R Wed 7 pm."

The FBI did not disclose this to the public right away. Behind the scenes, FBI agents searched furiously for "Nathan R." Around that time, explosives experts at the lab made a jaw-dropping discovery of their own. The bombs that had maimed Epstein and Gelernter were more powerful than the Unabomber's previous devices. He was now using a potent mixture of potassium chlorate and aluminum powder. This allowed him to pack much more dangerous explosives into smaller packages.

Years later, after Puckett had read the Unabomber's secret journals, she saw the workings of a tortured soul. He had taken the six years between attacks to perfect his bombs. He was most content, she said, when building them.

"You can view the painstaking evolution of his devices as a kind of therapy," Puckett said. "It was only when he was actively working on them that he didn't write about the torment he was suffering." Indeed, Puckett would eventually learn, he was achingly lonely.

Alone with his thoughts, the bomber had taught himself how to make deadly explosives. But he had picked a bad time to return as America's deadliest homegrown terrorist. The newly appointed attorney general of the United States, the top law enforcement official in the land, took her job very seriously. And she wanted the bomber brought to justice.

CHAPTER 6

Janet Reno, the first woman ever confirmed as attorney general, was a commanding presence. She stood six foot two, with strong shoulders and big eyeglasses. Reno supervised ninety-six thousand attorneys, federal agents, and other Justice Department employees—including those working for the FBI.

One of her first major decisions on the new job came in July 1993, when she ordered the FBI to head the UNABOM Task Force. Reno also ordered agents from two other agencies—the U.S. Postal Inspection Service and the Bureau of Alcohol, Tobacco, and Firearms—to serve on the task force, better known as the UTF.

The FBI soon discovered a major problem. Those three federal agencies had collected twelve million pages of case files, and they were scattered in offices all across the country. If you stacked those pages, they would stand four times higher than Chicago's Sears Tower—then the world's tallest building. The FBI had to buy a new computer system to store the records. Then the bureau did something groundbreaking: It built the FBI's very first website to help raise a reward in the UNABOM case. Building a website might not sound like a big deal today, with more than one billion websites on the internet. But back then, the World Wide Web was just two years old. Only one in five American households even owned a computer.

On October 6, 1993, newly appointed FBI Director Louis J. Freeh went on national TV. He announced a $1 million reward—some of it raised through the new FBI website—for information leading to the Unabomber's capture. Freeh encouraged tipsters to phone a toll-free hotline: 1-800-701-BOMB. Key members of the UTF then gave interviews to major news outlets, as well as to the popular TV series *America's Most Wanted*. But the UNABOM investigation soon stalled again as key agents were pulled off the team to work on new criminal cases.

Freeh decided the UNABOM probe needed a fresh approach. So he put the case in the hands of Jim R. Freeman, the special agent in charge of the FBI in San

Francisco. The City by the Bay would remain the permanent home of the UTF. The team would eventually take up the twelfth floor of the city's Phillip Burton Federal Building.

Puckett at that time was still working to catch Russian spies. But agents involved in the bombing case had invited her to UTF meetings to get her insights. Puckett knew that some agents thought the case was a loser. But she respected Freeman for attacking the problem head-on. Freeman had spent three decades investigating terrorists, spies, bank robbers, fugitives, kidnappers, armed drug dealers, and murderers. His mind still worked like that of a clever street agent.

In April 1994, Freeman picked Puckett's friend Terry Turchie to manage the day-to-day operations of the task force. Turchie was six feet tall and had a big grin that always made people wonder what he was thinking. He had spent most of his career protecting Americans from foreign spies, not catching criminals. In fact, he once wrestled a Soviet spy to the floor of a New York City subway platform, arresting him for espionage. Now Turchie would try to wrestle the UNABOM case to the ground, as well.

Turchie encouraged longtime investigators on the

case to throw out their pet theories. He wanted them to focus not on hunches, but on cold, hard facts. For example, agents knew that the Unabomber almost certainly found addresses for his victims in a public library. They also learned that the lone eyewitness in the case, Tammy Fluehe, had never been happy with the original sketch of the Unabomber.

Agent Donald Max Noel, the UTF's senior FBI agent, flew out to Utah with celebrated sketch artist Jeanne Boylan to meet with Fluehe. Noel, nicknamed "Mad Max" for his fiery temper, was smart, gruff, and opinionated. He was happy to learn that Fluehe had kept excellent notes from her 1987 encounter with the Unabomber. Noel recalled that as Fluehe helped Boylan create a better sketch of the bomber, he kept an

Forensic composite artist Jeanne Boylan worked with eyewitness Tammy Fluehe to create a more accurate sketch of the Unabomber.

eye on Fluehe's three-year-old in another room. The child and the tough-as-nails agent watched *The Lion King*. When Boylan was finished, Fluehe proclaimed the new sketch a much better resemblance to the Unabomber. Agents used the sketch to eliminate UNABOM suspects who did not look like him.

Turchie delighted in such breakthroughs. He thought the Unabomber, who had skillfully avoided capture for sixteen years, was as cunning as any spy he had ever come across. Just like a spy, the bomber used a code name—FC—and communicated with the FBI using an authentication code.

Only much later would Turchie and the task force learn that their bomber had taken other spylike steps to throw off his FBI pursuers. He wore disguises when he traveled. He donned a blond wig, which he wore under his hoodie. He used his collection of aviator sunglasses. Sometimes he changed his appearance by stuffing Kleenex, cotton, or chewing gum into his mouth and nostrils. He had constructed shoes that made his feet appear smaller than they really were. And at one point, he even collected blond hairs from a bus station lavatory and taped them on some of his

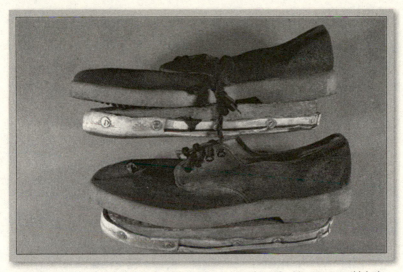

The bomber built a pair of shoes that he hoped would make his pursuers think the Unabomber had smaller feet than he did.

explosives. He wanted the FBI to believe he had light-colored hair.

In fact, the bomber's hair was brown, turning gray with age.

Even after Turchie had the UTF agents reexamine every fact in the case, he concluded that their analysis couldn't solve the bombings. He described the obstacles to their success like this: Each of the fourteen bombings had been like a thousand-piece jigsaw puzzle. Federal agents had dumped fourteen thousand pieces into one big pile, but had no photos of the completed puzzles to guide their work. Putting it all together was an almost impossible challenge.

One thing was certain: The agents needed better insights into their bomber's mind. Early on, they had gotten regular help from two of the FBI's elite profilers based in the bureau's Behavioral Analysis Unit in Quantico, Virginia. Now Turchie wanted them to write up a new profile of the kind of person likely to have committed the bombings.

On TV, Quantico's profilers seem to crawl right into their subjects' minds. They figure out their next moves and solve the crime in an hour-long show. Turchie knew that in real life, profilers aren't superhuman. All he wanted was an updated profile of the bomber based on his last few attacks. But his profilers told him their profile wouldn't change.

Why?

Because they believed Buckley Crist Jr., the professor whose return address had been on the package in that first mail-bomb attack in 1978, was the bomber. They believed Crist wanted to get back at a campus security officer who had once given him a traffic ticket. So, they reasoned, he plotted to injure the officer in a mail-bombing. Turchie thought their explanation was laughable, and he ordered them to update the profile. When they did, it still resembled Buckley Crist Jr.

Turchie branded them incompetent and sent them packing. Then he went looking for a new behavioral profiler.

CHAPTER 7

One day around Halloween in 1994, Kathy Puckett walked out of the federal building wearing a black raincoat. There she ran into Turchie, who had been looking for her. He asked what she was doing.

"I'm going to lunch at this great new place on the corner," she said. "Want to come along?"

The two old friends grabbed a table at Millennium, an expensive vegan restaurant where Puckett felt right at home. She ate no animal products. Turchie, on the other hand, struggled to make sense of the meatless menu. He was more of a Burger King guy.

Puckett had worked for Turchie from 1988 to 1990 on Squad 12, which targeted Soviet spies. He recalled her strengths as a spy hunter. She spoke Russian. She had studied Russian culture. She understood the strengths and weaknesses of Soviet spies. And perhaps more important, Puckett was a highly trained psychologist who understood how criminal minds work.

Turchie and Puckett had once teamed up on a major espionage case. Their subject was a Soviet Bloc spy. He had taken on a phony name and background to live illegally in the United States and spy on Americans. Turchie had asked Puckett, then working toward her PhD in clinical psychology, to write up a behavioral analysis of their subject. He was impressed by her report, which offered clues about what made the man tick. Their case was a major success, but it was so secret that even today, the FBI cannot talk about it.

Turchie, now seated in front of a confusing plate of veggies, got right to the point.

"I need you on the task force, Kathy."

Puckett tried not to show her excitement. She had hoped for a spot on the UTF for months after hearing endless talk about the mysteries of the case. Puckett knew that working for Turchie again would be fun and rewarding.

"I know what you can do," Turchie told her. "You proved it on Squad 12. You're also a team player, and I need that. I need to be able to rely on someone to be there for the agents and analysts when they develop suspects. I need fresh eyes on this. So . . . will you do it?"

Puckett grinned. "I'm already there."

On his way back to the office, Turchie picked up a cheeseburger.

Puckett thought Turchie was clever to include spy hunters on the UTF. "We were used to looking for needles in haystacks," she later recalled. And if ever there was a tiny needle hiding out in a huge haystack, it was the Unabomber.

Before her invitation to join the UTF, Puckett had given serious thought to quitting the FBI. She was disappointed in herself and her career. She wanted to be one of those agents who excelled, who solved the FBI's biggest puzzles, but her dreams hadn't worked out. So Puckett had taken steps to switch careers, earning her PhD in psychology while still working for the bureau. She daydreamed of becoming a licensed clinical psychologist.

But one vegan meal had changed all that.

Puckett charged into her true dream job: hunting for America's longest-running serial bomber. She pored over stacks of investigative files and evidence reports for behavioral clues about the bomber. She read and reread the letters he wrote to his victims and *The New York Times* for clues about his personality. Just a few weeks after joining the UTF, Puckett shared her insights with Turchie and key investigators on the team.

"Safety, security, and secrecy are of paramount importance to the Unabomber," she told them. She explained that the bomber had not planned his first few attacks very carefully. But over time, she said, the bombings and targets of his rage had grown more precise. In the last year, he had written anonymous letters to explain why he launched his campaign of bloodshed. He held himself up as a revolutionary—the public's protector against industry and technology. "In reality," Puckett explained, "he is simply seeking attention for himself."

She told her colleagues that the bomber's meticulous nature, and the pride he took in his explosives, reflected an obsessive-compulsive personality. He was very organized, a perfectionist. Control, Puckett said, meant everything to him. While he might appear to be calm and composed on the outside, this was only to prevent his deep anger and fear from bursting out and ruining everything.

Much later, the FBI would find a secret trove of the

Unabomber's writing. His own words confirmed Puckett's theories about their angry bomber:

"As you know," he wrote, "I have a good deal of anger in me and there are lots of people I'd like to hurt." The bomber explained that he had learned to turn his hatred against his greatest enemy: technology and organized society. "I am still plenty angry, you understand, but the difference is that I am now able to strike back, to a degree."

Puckett studied serial bombers of America's past to see if they had any common traits. The FBI had never actually done an analysis like this. She would have to break new ground to produce insights on this rare, terrifying brand of killer—the lone-wolf terrorist.

The most infamous of the nation's serial bombers was George Metesky, nicknamed the "Mad Bomber," who terrorized New York City from 1940 to 1956. Metesky was a mechanic. He held a red-hot grudge against his former employer, Consolidated Edison power company. He planted thirty-three bombs at company sites and in other spots across the city. Twenty-two of the explosives went off, injuring fifteen people.

Puckett saw parallels between Metesky and the Unabomber. Both wanted to punish people. Both wrote anonymous claims of responsibility. Both also took pains to authenticate their violence. Metesky had inserted the letters "F.P." in his bombs, later telling police they stood for "Fair Play." Puckett thought the Unabomber might have inserted "FC" into his explosives because he admired Metesky.

She would eventually learn the Mad Bomber and the Unabomber were very different men. Metesky lived in a city of nearly eight million people. The Unabomber hid all alone, five miles from the nearest town, shivering through some of America's coldest winters. Now and again, Puckett would learn, he boarded buses that took him to big cities.

Often on those trips, he carried a bomb.

CHAPTER 8

On the morning of December 10, 1994, Thomas J. Mosser was enjoying a quiet Saturday morning in his North Caldwell, New Jersey, home. The fifty-year-old advertising executive planned to take his family on a hunt for a Christmas tree later that day. He was in the kitchen with his wife, Susan Mosser, and their fifteen-month-old daughter Kelly when the toddler dashed away. Her mom chased her down in the living room.

Tom Mosser, alone in the kitchen, examined a package.

"I don't recognize the return address," he said, loud enough to be heard in the living room.

"Neither do I," Susan Mosser replied.

The next sound she heard was a monstrous explosion. It came from the kitchen, on the other side of a wall.

Susan grabbed Kelly in her arms and fled to the lawn outside, where she called 911. Then she reentered their home, finding a mist of powder hanging in the air. She made her way through the ruins of her kitchen and found Tom Mosser on the floor. He lay on his back, his face blackened by the explosion.

Susan saw that his chest was covered in blood. She leaped for a towel, instead grabbing a colorful baby blanket covered in ducklings. She knelt and spread the blanket over her husband.

"You're going to be okay, Tom. Help is coming."

He moaned.

"I love you, Tom."

Susan soon felt the hands of a firefighter plucking her to her feet. The smell of leaking gas filled the kitchen, and he needed to move her outside for safety.

Behind them, Thomas Mosser lay dead.

A short while later, nearly three thousand miles away, Turchie picked up the phone. On the line was an FBI official in New Jersey, who ran down the basics of the bombing. When Turchie got off the phone, he paged Special Agent in Charge Jim Freeman, who was playing golf at Half Moon Bay, a coastal town south of San Francisco.

"Terry, what's up?"

"Jim, we've had another bombing."

Later that day, the UTF's primary explosives expert at the lab in Quantico phoned Turchie.

"It's UNABOM," he said.

Inside the package mailed from San Francisco on December 3 was a white cardboard box that in turn held a homemade wooden box. Inside that box was an aluminum pipe bomb filled with razor blades and green one-inch nails. When Mosser opened the box, nails had been fired into his heart and brain.

In January 1995, FBI Director Louis Freeh paid a visit to the San Francisco office.

Agents on the UNABOM Task Force warmly greeted their director, who had served as an FBI agent just like them. Freeh also knew about serial bombers. While serving as a government prosecutor, he had built the criminal case against Walter LeRoy Moody Jr., whose bombs killed a judge and a civil rights lawyer.

"I've discussed the UTF strategy with Jim Freeman and Terry Turchie here, and it's a good one," Freeh told the team. He pointed out that luck did not solve cases like UNABOM—good strategies and determination did. Freeh glanced around the room for questions.

Max Noel, selected by other agents to point out problems the UTF faced, was the first to raise his hand. Turchie knew he could count on Noel to offer an opinion or two. Turchie had always encouraged members of the team to speak the truth, and, to his credit, Noel spoke his mind while toning down the "Mad Max" attitude for the director. But he did not hold back, launching a series of complaints.

For one, he said, the FBI's other field offices had ignored the UTF's requests for assistance. One example was the team's nationwide request for help running down leads about the "Call Nathan R" note. Agents in those offices, working to solve their own cases, had offered little to no help. Noel complained that agents at the FBI had dragged their feet, taking forever to turn grainy surveillance photos of a shadowy figure at a San Francisco post office into sharper images. And, he said, Quantico's profilers never completed a review of UNABOM crime scenes. The UTF needed cooperation.

Freeh listened intently to those and other criticisms. The next day, Turchie learned that the FBI director wanted the case solved and had pledged his full support. As evidence, Quantico's behavioral profiling unit transferred profiler James "Fitz" Fitzgerald to the UTF. Turchie paired Fitz with Puckett. Together, he hoped, they would climb into the mind of the bomber.

That spring, antigovernment extremists detonated a two-ton bomb in Oklahoma City that killed 168 people, including nineteen children. FBI officials worried that the Unabomber might have played a role in that attack. Puckett quickly set them straight. The bombing in Oklahoma was mass murder aimed at a wide range of people. The Unabomber, she explained, typically picked individual victims. The Oklahoma bombing simply wasn't his style.

Police in Oklahoma caught those bombers quickly. While Puckett and other members of the UTF applauded the swift arrests, their bomber had now been on the loose for nearly seventeen years. He continued to taunt them, mailing bombs from San Francisco—right under their noses.

CHAPTER 9

Kathy Puckett had been on the UNABOM case for less than six months when the bomber killed for the third time. The package bomb that rocked the California Forestry Association on April 24, 1995, left Gil Murray's wife and two sons grieving his death. That very night, eighteen-year-old Wilson Murray was to accept an award for his sports and classroom successes. Gil Murray, bursting with pride, had planned to be there.

Instead, a coroner solemnly moved his body from the bombing scene.

That very day, a new letter from the Unabomber reached *The New York Times*. His message ran to 1,700 words. For the first time, he explained how he targeted his victims, and why he felt the urge to kill.

"We blew up Thomas Mosser last December because he was a Burston-Marsteller executive," the bomber wrote, misspelling the name Burson. He wrote that Burson-Marsteller was a public relations firm that helped large companies manage their images. The bomber claimed that Mosser's PR company had helped the oil and gas company Exxon rebuild its public image after one of its oil tankers—the *Exxon Valdez*—struck a reef in Alaska and dumped 10.8 million gallons of crude oil into the water. The spill killed hundreds of thousands of sea otters, harbor seals, seabirds, and other species. The bomber hated the PR firm because he thought it had controlled people's minds by making Exxon look better after the massive spill.

The bomber's letter also explained why FC's explosives went to universities. He was not angry with all professors, he wrote. But he wanted to punish experts in the computer sciences, genetics, and psychology for "all this growth and progress garbage." FC's goal, he wrote, was to destroy modern industrial society. He believed humans should live simply, in small groups, making their own rules. He hoped FC's bombings would inspire others.

Then the bomber offered the *Times* a chance to stop

the bloodshed. He promised to quit mailing bombs if the newspaper would publish an article that FC had written. He made clear that the piece ran at least twenty-nine thousand words (longer than this book). He promised he would resume bombing if the police closed in on him. Also, he reserved the right—even after the publication of the article—to commit sabotage. That meant he would still terrorize people, but not kill them. The bomber told the *Times* to publish its reply in the daily paper. If the newspaper agreed to print the manuscript, he would type a final version of his essay and mail it to the newspaper for publication.

"If the answer is unsatisfactory," he wrote, "we will start building our next bomb."

The bomber's threat angered Puckett and her FBI colleagues. The United States had a long-standing policy of never giving in to the demands of terrorists. The government did not negotiate with anyone who made such threats. Neither did news organizations such as the *Times*.

Yet this terrorist, the Unabomber, was a proven killer. They knew his bombs were only getting more powerful. If they ignored his demands, he would probably kill again and again.

But what could they do? What *should* they do?

The *Times* handed over the bomber's letter to the FBI. Agents dusted it for fingerprints but got nothing.

Puckett knew the real clues were the bomber's own words. She studied his new letter for hints about his personality. She believed the long essay he promised to send the *Times* was a potential game changer. It showed that he craved attention. Finally, he was coming out of the shadows. He was taking risks. Puckett felt this opened a door for the UTF to hunt him down.

The bomber had mailed five items on April 20, 1995. One was the letter to the *Times*, which explained for the first time that "FC" stood for "Freedom Club." Another was the package that killed Murray. Two more letters went to a pair of Nobel Prize–winning genetics researchers, warning them to stop their work. The other was received by David Gelernter, the computer scientist disfigured in the 1993 Yale bombing.

"People with advanced degrees aren't as smart as they think they are," the bomber wrote to Gelernter. "If you'd had any brains you would have realized that there are a lot of people out there who resent bitterly the way techno-nerds like you are changing the world and you wouldn't have been dumb enough to open an unexpected package from an unknown source."

The Unabomber mailed six more letters on June 24, 1995. He sent copies of his article—"Industrial Society and Its Future"—to *The New York Times*, *The Washington Post*, a men's magazine, and Tom R. Tyler, a Berkeley psychology professor. At 34,649 words, the text was even longer than the bomber had predicted. The bomber also mailed a copy to *Scientific American*. The sixth letter, received by the *San Francisco Chronicle*, did not include a copy of the article.

But its contents would panic the nation.

On the afternoon of Wednesday, June 28, 1995, Jim Freeman took a call in San Francisco from an editor at the *Chronicle*. The editor claimed the newspaper had received a letter from FC, and he was threatening mass murder. Freeman and Turchie hurried to the *Chronicle* office to inspect the letter. The return address was 549 Wood Street, Woodlake, CA 93286.

The two FBI supervisors read the sender's name: Frederick Benjamin Isaac Wood. The first letters of the sender's name spelled "F.B.I." The bomber was taunting them. "While it's a crime to assault an FBI agent," Turchie would later recall, "it is not a crime to insult one. But boy, does it make us that much more determined."

The letter began: "WARNING. The terrorist group FC,

called unabomber by the FBI, is planning to blow up an airliner out of Los Angeles International Airport some time during the next six days."

Freeman and Turchie knew all about the Unabomber's 1979 attempt to down American Airlines Flight 444. They had no reason to believe he was anything but serious. So they scrambled to alert the FBI's law enforcement partners.

Soon, hundreds of agents, police officers, and sheriff's deputies rallied at an airport command post. FBI teams inspected nearly two hundred truckloads of mail before it was loaded onto planes. Federal Aviation Administration workers asked travelers if they had packed their own bags or let them out of their sight.

Meanwhile, Puckett and the team's new profiler,

WARNING

The terrorist group FC, called unabomber by the FBI, is planning to blow up an airliner out of Los Angeles International Airport some time during the next six days. To prove that the writer of this letter knows something about FC, the first two digits of their identifying number are 55.

The Unabomber typed this note to the San Francisco Chronicle, *warning that he would blow up an airliner within the next six days.*

James Fitzgerald, retreated to a quiet spot in the office to read, and reread, the Unabomber's latest letters.

Safety precautions at LAX disrupted airmail and delayed flights. But thankfully, no bombs went off. The next day, on June 29, *The New York Times* received another letter from the Unabomber. It read, "Since the public has a short memory, we decided to play one last prank to remind them who we are. But, no, we haven't tried to plant a bomb on an airline (recently)." The bomber went on to say that he was glad his 1979 bomb had not killed innocent people aboard Flight 444.

"We don't think it is necessary to do any public soul-searching in this letter," the bomber wrote. "But we will say that we are not insensitive to the pain caused by our bombings."

Puckett studied those words. She noted that the bomber, for the first time, seemed to express compassion for his victims. It was clear to her that he was trying to pass himself off as the champion of innocent people, taking aim at those he found guilty of pushing technology upon the world. He had already killed three people, but Puckett knew he didn't consider himself a murderer.

He thought of himself as an executioner for the good of humanity.

At a meeting with UTF leaders, Puckett held up a copy of one of the bomber's letters. She noted that he had promised to stop his terrorism if the manifesto was published.

"I don't believe that he can actually do this, even if he wants to," she said. "It's just not possible for him to stop the bombings. . . . He's a bomber and will continue to bomb. He can't help it. Bombs don't have boundaries."

CHAPTER 10

Puckett and Fitzgerald obtained copies of the Unabomber manifesto and launched themselves into a grueling homework assignment. They read every word of the manuscript. Then they read it again. And again, and again. With each read, they found new insights into the bomber's thinking. They grew so familiar with the manuscript that they sometimes woke with the bomber's words in their heads. Puckett could recite the opening sentence from memory: "The Industrial Revolution and its consequences have been a disaster for the human race."

As Puckett and Fitzgerald pored through the text—pounded out on an old Smith Corona typewriter—they saw themes. The Unabomber believed that inventions in the 1800s, such as railroads, telegraphs, and steamboats, had made life easier for Americans, but taken them away from nature. He believed that modern society robbed people of their freedoms, leaving them stressed out and unfulfilled. "We therefore advocate a revolution," he wrote, "against the industrial system."

Reading between the lines of the manifesto, Puckett and Fitzgerald discovered a recurring theme. The bomber wrote a lot about children. He believed technology had changed the way grownups brought them up, schooled them, and helped shape them into adults. The bomber also believed that humans who lost touch with nature grew more violent.

"This whole thing is biographical," Puckett recalled saying at the time. "He doesn't realize it, but he's giving us a portrait of his interior self. And somebody is going to recognize him by these words."

During a task force meeting, Fitzgerald told the team that his behavioral colleagues back at Quantico had also analyzed the manifesto.

"Whoever wrote the manuscript has taken years to develop his belief system," Fitzgerald said. "The manuscript represents how he feels, and he's probably felt this way for some time. We think the paper is well written, and that he sounds like a social scientist. He may have shared his themes with others, and publication might help someone recognize his words and come forward. . . . As you know, we believe that he'll stop bombing if his manuscript is published."

Puckett bristled. She told the team that Fitzgerald and his Quantico pals were out to lunch if they thought the bomber would quit bombing. She agreed that the bomber had arrived at his views long before. She thought that when he wrote about depression, low self-esteem, and emptiness, he was describing himself. She also agreed with Fitzgerald that the most prevalent topic in the manifesto was the way society treats children.

"What other themes do you see?" Turchie asked.

"Besides children," she said, "he writes about feelings of inferiority, job requirements and conditions, industrial labor, psychological problems, alcoholism, sex, and love."

Freeman wanted to know how any of that might help the UTF capture the guy.

Like Fitzgerald, Puckett thought that if a major publication printed the manifesto, someone would recognize the bomber's words or the way he expressed himself. Few people wrote so venomously about the evils of technology. Puckett also thought that the more the UTF studied his words, the more they would learn about his personality.

Some of the UTF's agents, including the outspoken Max Noel, thought focusing on the bomber's words might be a mistake.

"I think we have to be careful to stick with the facts," Noel said during a team meeting. He was concerned that the UTF was putting too much weight on the manifesto. Some agents on the team thought the Unabomber might have written the essay as a red herring—a false lead to throw off his pursuers.

Puckett strongly disagreed. She felt that the bomber's words were authentic and offered the FBI a good chance of finding him. Once the FBI found a suspect, she and other agents could link events in the bomber's life with the themes in his writing. With any luck, their work would prove they had the right guy.

On a blustery Wednesday in July 1995, the FBI's deputy director, Bill Esposito, strode into the San Francisco Field Office with a handful of the bureau's senior executives. They joined the UTF in a conference room to discuss the task force's progress since the bomber had released his manifesto.

Turchie told them that the manifesto mentioned four books by name. The UTF had learned that one of the books, *The Ancient Engineers*, had been required reading for about seventy students at Northwestern University—site of the Unabomber's first attacks. Agents planned to interview every one of those students. Agents were trying to determine whether the other texts had been in use at any of the eight universities targeted by the Unabomber.

Esposito posed a question to Turchie.

"What do you need to bring this case to an end?"

The question surprised Turchie. Government agencies such as the FBI were always trying to save money, not spend it. But here was the FBI's second-highest-ranking official asking him for a wish list. Turchie told Esposito that the UTF was composed of one squad of about twenty FBI agents, five postal inspectors, and three ATF agents. The task force, he said, needed three squads—one to investigate suspects, another to reinvestigate the bombings, and a third to manage the huge number of tips pouring into the UTF's toll-free tip line.

Turchie said they also needed fifty analysts to comb through data.

Esposito left the room and returned a short time later.

"I spoke with the director," he announced. "We're transferring fifty agents ... to staff three UNABOM squads. . . . We're transferring in as many analysts as we can move, hopefully somewhere between twenty-five and fifty on a rotating basis, thirty days at a time. We're also giving you more money to staff a twenty-four-hour 1-800 number with multiple lines. Anything else you need?"

Esposito had just delivered an early Christmas to the UTF. As a bonus, he promoted Turchie to assistant special agent in charge.

"Now," Esposito growled, "solve this damn case, would you?"

Chapter II

The Unabomber gave the American press a deadline. In a letter to *The New York Times*, he demanded that a major publication print his manifesto—or announce plans to publish it—by September 24, 1995.

Otherwise, as promised, he would renew his campaign of bombing and bloodshed.

Puckett and her colleagues debated what to do. She repeated her core beliefs about the culprit, including that the Unabomber couldn't keep himself from bombing, and that publication of the manifesto offered the FBI a chance to catch the killer.

After much soul-searching and a few arguments, the UTF decided to push for publication of the manifesto.

On a sticky summer day in 1995, Puckett, Freeman, and Turchie passed through the doors of FBI headquarters. The sprawling J. Edgar Hoover Building occupied a busy corner several blocks from the White House. Puckett and her colleagues soon took seats at a conference table teeming with FBI executives in dark suits. Director Freeh took a seat at the head of the table. Soon, all eyes turned to Turchie.

"We're recommending publication because we feel it represents the lifelong work and philosophy of the Unabomber," Turchie told the executives. "We think someone might recognize it and call the 1-800 hotline."

Turchie said that printing the essay in *The Washington Post* offered a unique chance to catch the bomber. He explained the *Post* was not widely circulated in the American West. So the plan was to send agents to the few newsstands that sold the newspaper on the day it was published. On the morning that the *Post*'s manifesto edition hit the streets, undercover agents would go to those newsstands to see who bought them. Turchie believed the bomber might buy a trophy copy for himself.

One of the FBI's leading criminal profilers also

addressed Freeh and other senior executives. He said Quantico's Behavioral Science Unit believed the Unabomber cherished his credibility and would not bomb again if the manifesto was published.

Freeh asked Puckett for her thoughts.

"Here's where I disagree with my colleagues at Quantico," she said. "We aren't convinced he truly intends to stop bombing if he's published. He may not be able to stop, even if he wants to. This is what he does, and it defines him. So, although the *Times* and the *Post* would like a guarantee that by publishing him they'll stop him from bombing, we can't give it to them. The reason to publish is exactly what Terry said. He's left us no other path that leads to him for almost twenty years. We believe that publishing his manifesto will cause someone who knows him to come forward and identify him to us."

Freeh nodded his approval, and Puckett was glad to see that. But she knew the FBI now had to sell the idea to the attorney general.

The next day, Puckett lugged her briefcase, her pocketbook, and an armload of files across Pennsylvania Avenue, high heels clopping on the street as she walked, accompanied by Freeman, Turchie, and Director Freeh himself to brief Janet Reno. Freeh, noticing Puckett's heavy load, offered to carry her briefcase. But she just rolled her eyes and grinned.

"Like I'd ever live *that* down!" she said.

Puckett took a seat in a Justice Department conference room and watched with awe as Attorney General Janet Reno walked into the room. Reno took a seat and leaned in toward the table to hear what Turchie had to say.

Turchie explained that the FBI had toiled for many years to catch the Unabomber. But in all that time, agents had not obtained a single piece of evidence that could identify him. The bomber had left no reliable fingerprints or DNA. None of the debris left from the bombs could be traced back to where it had been purchased.

Reno now turned to Puckett to hear the latest behavioral analysis of the bomber. Puckett told her that he valued academic success, might live in the country, and probably used libraries for reference materials. She said the manifesto seemed to be autobiographical. She said there was no guarantee that publishing his words would stop the bombings, but that taking the bomber's thoughts to the public offered a chance that someone would recognize them and step forward.

Puckett and her superiors recommended to Reno that she ask *The Washington Post* to publish the manifesto. Reno and Freeh walked out of the room to confer, returning moments later with smiles and handshakes. They would meet the next morning with top executives of the *Times* and the *Post*, whose publications—like news organizations everywhere—had been covering the grim Unabomber saga very closely.

America's newspapers are fiercely independent. They report *on* the government, not *to* the government. Yet here they were together in the FBI director's conference room—Freeh, Reno, and top executives of America's two most prestigious newspapers, *The Washington Post* and *The New York Times*. Freeman and Turchie, representing the UTF, also sat in on the meeting. Not one person in the room wanted a terrorist telling them what to do. But together they would have to decide how to respond to the bomber's demands.

Freeh sensed tension in the room. The journalists in front of him were sometimes extremely critical of the FBI.

"Thanks for coming," he said with a grin. "We don't see each other often enough."

The room came apart with laughter.

Publishers of the *Times* and the *Post* got right down to business. They wanted to know if the FBI thought they should publish the manifesto.

"Absolutely," Freeh said. "We strongly believe that publication of the manifesto will attract the attention of the whole country. Because of that, we believe someone who knows the Unabomber will recognize the words and content as his, and will be moved to turn him in."

Editors of the *Post* and the *Times* worried that publishing the manifesto might open the door to printing the words of every lunatic with a cause. They didn't want to be accused of acting as an arm of the government. They also knew that if they published the bomber's words and he bombed again, the public would be furious with them. They wondered aloud what they would tell readers if that happened.

Reno spoke right up.

"You can say that the attorney general of the United States and the director of the FBI wanted the manifesto published, asked that you publish it, and that I, Janet Reno, accept full and complete responsibility for whatever happens as a result of the publication."

The newspapers agreed to jointly publish the manifesto.

CHAPTER 12

On Tuesday, September 19, 1995, the *Post* printed the bomber's manifesto, with the *Times* sharing the costs. Critics immediately slammed the newspapers, accusing them of rewarding a terrorist. "It inspires dozens of wannabe killers," one crime expert told the *Times*. "This is like turning over a newspaper at gunpoint," said the editor of the *American Journalism Review*. But one terrorism authority offered a different view:

"It is better to spill ink than to spill blood."

The FBI's plan was to stake out newsstands in the American West to see if the Unabomber could be caught buying a souvenir copy. Back then, the *Post* circulated more than eight hundred thousand copies of its daily newspaper. The FBI believed the Unabomber probably lived in the western half of the United States.

In San Francisco, fifty FBI employees awoke hours before dawn. They dressed in street clothes, casually blending in at newsstands as patrons purchased the *Post*. Agents looked at each person who bought a copy, comparing their face to that in the Unabomber sketch. One by one, agents ruled them out as suspects.

Then came a man in his sixties carrying a briefcase. He bought a copy of the *Post* from a newsstand called Harold's. A pair of agents followed him as he boarded a train and then a bus and made his way home. Agents, aware the man had ties to radical groups, knocked on his apartment door. He eyed them suspiciously, but allowed the agents in. His dwelling was full of yellowed newspapers. The agents perked up when he told them he was against technology and thought the FBI was following him. But like thousands of other suspects across America—including a minister, a dog musher, and a masseur—the man was ruled out as the Unabomber.

As the manifesto hit the streets, the UTF's toll-free hotline lit up. The line would eventually log more than fifty-three thousand calls. Many tipsters, angling for the $1 million reward, phoned to say the bomber was their ex-husband, their brother, or an in-law. But all were ruled out as suspects.

Puckett wasn't discouraged. There was no time for that. Innocent lives were still in jeopardy because the bomber was still out there. She and her fellow agents did not have the luxury of feeling sorry for themselves. They pressed ahead, focused on finding the killer.

"When you are on the hunt," she said, "you're the hunter."

Not long after the *Post* published the Unabomber manifesto, a Washington lawyer named Anthony "Tony" Bisceglie contacted the FBI. He told an agent that one of his clients had a twenty-three-page essay written in 1971 by his brother that sounded a bit like the manifesto.

In San Francisco, Supervisory Special Agent Joel Moss, hip-deep in suspect files, arranged for an agent in Washington to go to the lawyer's office to pick up the essay.

On a Wednesday in early February 1996, Moss heard a voice blaring from an overhead speaker in the UTF bullpen: "Will someone from the UNABOM Task Force please call the switchboard?" Moss looked around the carpeted bullpen full of desks and file cabinets. When none of his colleagues picked up, he reached for the phone and soon found himself on the line with Washington Special Agent Molly Flynn.

Flynn told Moss she had picked up the twenty-three-page essay from Tony Bisceglie and taken it to the FBI Laboratory. An agent there had looked it over and said it didn't match the Unabomber manifesto. But Flynn had also read the manifesto and the essay. She thought they sounded similar. So she promised to fax Moss the essay to see what he thought.

A half hour later, the fax landed on Moss's cluttered desk, where it sat for hours. At about 6 P.M., he picked up the papers and began to read. Certain phrases jumped right out at him. Moss placed the essay next to the manifesto. The typefaces were different, but some of the language and ideas were similar. The more he read, the more excited he got. A thought crossed his mind: *I don't know his name yet. But I'm the first to know for certain that we've found the Unabomber.*

Moss phoned Puckett, an old friend, and told her he had something she should read. A short time later, sitting in a coffee shop near the FBI office, Moss watched Puckett's expression as she read the essay. The words seemed to be sucking the breath out of her. Then, she abruptly looked up from the paper.

"Where did you get this?"

Moss didn't answer right away. He let the gravity of the essay sink in. Then he asked Puckett what she thought.

She looked down at the paper.

"Well," she said, "this is the first thing I've seen in a year and a half that's made the hair on the back of my neck stand up."

Moss waited until the next morning, when his boss returned to the office, to ask him to join him for lunch at Max's Opera Café. He said Puckett was also coming.

"Can't," Turchie told him. He was lunching with Freeman.

Moss told him to get out of his meal with their boss. Turchie could tell something was up. He canceled with Freeman and, as the lunch hour approached, grabbed Noel. The two veteran agents walked into Max's, a place both knew well. Turchie had popped in during trying times for the comforting Russian cabbage soup. They grabbed seats at a table in the middle of the café, where Moss and Puckett soon joined them. Moss took his seat and pushed copies of the new essay in front of Turchie and Noel.

"We have a new suspect," he announced.

"What's this?" asked Turchie, sounding exhausted. It had been a trying week on the task force as agents worked nonstop on tips that went nowhere. Turchie and Noel felt whipped.

"We think this was written by the Unabomber," Puckett said.

"Well," Noel growled, "I hope it is, Kath. I hope it's the guy. But it's just a stack of paper to me, and not evidence of anything."

Moss turned to Turchie and asked him to give the essay a glance at home.

That evening, Turchie reclined on his couch to read the essay as his wife, Joy, watched a TV comedy. Turchie's eyes fell on five words . . . "the sphere of human freedom." He remembered that phrase. He had seen it in the Unabomber's manifesto. He looked at his wife, heart thumping with excitement.

"Joy," he said, "I think we've found the Unabomber."

She waved her hand in the air, not wanting him to interrupt the show.

"You didn't hear me," he said. "I think we've found the Unabomber."

"What?"

Assistant Special Agent in Charge Terry Turchie (middle) is flanked by Agents Joel Moss and Kathy Puckett. Turchie's wife, Joy, nicknamed the trio of spy hunters the "Three Musketeers."

Turchie told her about the new essay, about how it sounded like the manifesto.

"Seriously?"

Turchie grabbed his copy of the manifesto and flipped through the pages. And there, in the ninety-third paragraph, he found it: "We are going to argue that industrial-technological society cannot be reformed in such a way as to prevent it from progressively narrowing the sphere of human freedom. . . ."

Bingo.

CHAPTER 13

The following Saturday, key members of the UTF gathered around a speakerphone in Freeman's comfortable office suite. They listened in as Freeman chatted with Tony Bisceglie, telling the Washington lawyer that the UTF was intrigued by the twenty-three-page essay. He explained that a side-by-side comparison of the essay and the Unabomber manifesto had convinced them to investigate the essay's author.

Bisceglie explained that his client, whom he revealed only as "Dave," wanted to protect his brother. Dave's great hope was that the FBI could rule out his brother as the bomber. At the same time, Dave felt that if his brother was the Unabomber, someone had to stop him. Agents listened carefully as Bisceglie provided background on

Dave's brother, Ted, whom he described as a math genius.

Puckett and other task force members wanted to hear more about Ted. Bisceglie explained that Ted had grown up in the Chicago area. He had gone to Harvard University at age sixteen and later earned a PhD in mathematics from the University of Michigan. He had also taught at Berkeley. After a few years, he had moved back in with his parents in Chicago. Later, the socially awkward Ted developed a crush on the only woman he had ever kissed. She soon lost interest in him, and Ted moved to Salt Lake City. Then, in 1971, Ted bought 1.4 acres in Montana and built a small cabin, where he still lived. The place had no running water, gas, or electricity.

This information stunned the UTF. This "Ted"— whoever he was—had lived in or near the scenes of ten UNABOM attacks.

Bisceglie continued: "Dave knows that Ted has an old manual typewriter in the cabin, and a bicycle he uses to get to the nearby town. Dave also feels that Ted resembles the rough drawing of the Unabomber." Bisceglie then let the UTF know that Dave would provide no more information until the FBI gave him some assurances.

Dave wanted a promise that if Ted *was* the Unabomber, he wouldn't get the death penalty.

"Come on, Tony," Freeman said. "You know we can't do that." He explained to the lawyer that they needed more information on Ted, starting with his full name. But Bisceglie wouldn't budge. So Freeman came up with a compromise: The FBI was willing to pledge, in a letter, that it would take into consideration Dave's help if Ted was the Unabomber. The letter would specifically note that Dave did not want his brother put to death.

Bisceglie said he would await the letter.

Moss opened an investigation of "Ted," identifying him as suspect number 2,416. Agents pored through the massive UNABOM database and found a former Berkeley math professor named Theodore John Kaczynski, born in Chicago on May 22, 1942. Kaczynski kept a post office box in the tiny mountain town of Lincoln, Montana.

Bisceglie phoned Freeman.

"Okay, Jim," he said, "I discussed everything with my client. Pending receipt of your letter, he and his wife can meet with your agents this coming weekend in Washington, D.C. He has agreed to provide whatever help he can so that you can [rule out] his brother as the Unabomber."

In 1967, Theodore Kaczynski, at age 25, became the youngest assistant professor ever to teach math at the University of California, Berkeley.

After the meeting, Freeman and Turchie poured themselves cups of coffee and took seats in the conference room.

"Okay," Freeman said, "do you really think it's him?"

"Yes," Turchie said. "I do think we're closing in."

Chapter 14

Supervisors of the UNABOM Task Force assigned Kathy Puckett, agent Lee Stark, and another investigator to interview the family of suspect number 2,416: Theodore J. Kaczynski.

Puckett and Stark flew to Washington in the middle of February 1996. There, they joined other agents who would accompany them to the interview with Bisceglie and his clients, a married couple now identified as David Kaczynski and Linda Patrik. Kaczynski and Patrik lived in upstate New York, where David worked in a shelter for runaway and homeless children. Linda was a college professor.

Stark was the first to meet with the Kaczynskis, and things didn't go well. The couple seemed to be having second thoughts about talking to the FBI. On the bright side, David Kaczynski handed over forty-five letters that his older brother, Ted, had written to him.

Puckett knew that gaining Kaczynski and Patrik's confidence was crucial to the investigation. She had spent much of her career getting people to trust her with their secrets. The best way to get them talking, she knew, was to put them at ease. Puckett booked a large, comfortable suite for their meeting the next morning. She also arranged for a breakfast table of hot drinks, fresh fruit, and pastries.

The next morning, Puckett greeted Bisceglie, a short, dark-haired man in a tailored suit and black cowboy boots. The lawyer introduced them to his clients. David Kaczynski was a tall, lean man with a soft voice and a gentle face that betrayed his deep sorrows. Linda was petite with big, dark eyes. Puckett could see that Linda was ill at ease talking with the FBI, so she encouraged her guests and fellow agents to grab warm drinks and relax. She waited until the moment was right to begin the interview.

Linda was determined to help despite her discomfort. She told the agents how she and David came to contact the FBI. The previous August she'd been in Paris on sabbatical and happened to pick up a copy of the

International Herald Tribune. The newspaper carried a story about the Unabomber that included snippets from the manifesto. The story described the bomber as a loner, probably from Chicago, and familiar with Salt Lake City and Northern California. Linda knew that Ted Kaczynski had lived in all those places. While she had never met Ted, who had shunned her, she knew about his hatred of technology. Linda thought some of the ideas expressed by the Unabomber sounded like Ted.

"The article said the entire manuscript was going to be published," Linda told the agents. "I knew I wanted David to read it, in case Ted really was involved."

Linda recalled David meeting her in Paris, one of the world's most romantic cities. She deliberately did not bring up the Unabomber story the first night he was there. Instead, they enjoyed dinner on the balcony of their hotel. The next morning, Linda approached her husband.

"David," she said, "don't be angry with me. Has it ever occurred to you, even as a remote possibility, that your brother might be the Unabomber?"

"What?" he replied.

David suddenly felt defensive about Ted. He thought

his wife had let her imagination get away from her. He reminded Linda that Ted had never been violent and hated to travel. At that time, as David would later recall in his book, *Every Last Tie*, he could not imagine his own brother, whom he had idolized in their childhood, as a murderous bomber. But he promised his wife that when the manifesto was published, he would read it.

About a month later, the couple pulled up the manifesto on a library computer. After just a few minutes, a phrase leaped out at David: "cool-headed logicians." He recalled that Ted had once put him down for not being a "cool-headed logician."

David was so distraught that he wrote to Ted, voicing concerns about his brother's well-being. Ted's response staggered David like a punch to the gut. I DON'T EVER WANT TO SEE YOU OR HEAR FROM YOU, OR ANY OTHER MEMBER OF OUR FAMILY, AGAIN."

About this time, Linda passed two of Ted's letters to a language expert, who studied them. The expert concluded that there was a good chance that the author of the letters also wrote the manifesto. David and Linda later shared their concerns with Bisceglie.

Now in the hotel suite, Puckett looked at David. He

sat in a soft chair looking mournful. It was snowing outside, but warm in the room. She could only imagine how awful it must be to suspect—even a little—that your own brother might be the Unabomber. But now, Puckett had a job to do.

"We need to know as much as possible about your brother," she said. "So I'll be asking a lot of questions about your experiences and perceptions as you grew up together. What Ted was like at various ages. What his interests were. What his relationships with other people were like."

David told Puckett a long, painful story. He explained that Ted was a troubled man who preferred to be alone. His big brother had grown angry and bitter as he aged, cutting himself off from his family. In letters, he was cruel to his parents and to David. Later, their dad learned he had a deadly cancer and shot himself to death. Ted had not bothered to fly home for the funeral.

David wiped tears from his eyes, and Puckett talked to him in a soft voice.

"A lot of this is hard to talk about, and we know that," she said. "You need to take a break, so we'll stop for a while."

Puckett walked out to the balcony, where Bisceglie joined her to smoke a cigarette. She had once been a smoker, too, but had given up the bad habit.

"That was well done," he told her. "We're going to have to talk about what you're going to do next. I know how these things can go, and we have to make something clear. There will be no operational use of my clients in this investigation."

This meant David and Linda refused to take an active role in the FBI's probe of Ted Kaczynski. The couple would provide information about Ted, but they would not lure him into a trap.

When the interview resumed, Puckett pulled out several of Ted's letters to David. Some of his words sounded like the Unabomber. In one letter, for instance, Ted asked David to check suppliers and prices on sodium chloride—a chemical used in some of the bombings. Ted's letters also mentioned two books, including *The Ancient Engineers*, mentioned in the manifesto.

David told Puckett that he felt terrible for the Unabomber's victims and their families. But he also worried the FBI might get into a shootout with Ted and kill his brother.

"I have to do something," David told the agents. "But I have to protect Ted as much as I can. And I will do everything I can to help you to eliminate him as a suspect."

David said his mother, Wanda Kaczynski, also had letters from Ted. But David, protective of his mom, told Puckett he did not want agents to approach her until he could prepare her for the FBI's visit. Puckett would soon learn that David, too, had more of Ted's letters. He kept them in his remote cabin in West Texas, where he had long found peace, solitude, and great beauty.

Puckett knew any letter that Ted had mailed—to David, Wanda, or anyone else—would be helpful in the FBI's investigation. If a postmark on a letter showed Ted was in one city when the Unabomber was leaving a bomb in another, agents might be able to eliminate him as a suspect. But Puckett suspected Ted's letters would give them something else.

More evidence against Ted.

CHAPTER 15

At sunup on the last Saturday in February, a gleaming Chevy Suburban was gunned out of El Paso, Texas, onto Interstate 10. Its driver, a young, macho FBI agent, mashed the accelerator to the floor of the SUV, which now hurtled at a hundred miles per hour through the Chihuahuan Desert. The landscape teemed with cacti and rattlesnakes.

The FBI had put a small plane in the air to shadow the Chevy. Bureau officials were not worried about the armed agents inside the speeding Suburban. They were making sure no one harmed America's most important witness, David Kaczynski. He sat in the backseat with Puckett, who assured him that the plane droning overhead was standard procedure. Stark sat in the front passenger seat, nervously gripping the shoulder harness of his seat belt.

They were speeding to David's cabin near Terlingua, Texas, which sat on a patch of land he had bought years earlier to get away from it all. The Chevy crawled over steep rocks and parked. Puckett could see the cabin off in the scrub. They got out and walked the rest of the way.

Puckett was impressed with David's little hideaway. Inside were tidy bookshelves and colorful rugs. Sunlight poured onto the floors. David had lived stretches of his life here. He seemed happy to return, even under such grim circumstances. After a time, he walked outside and opened a trapdoor in the ground. He pulled out a stack of his brother's letters and handed them to the agents. Stark took them to a nearby table, where he catalogued them into evidence.

Inside the cabin, David put water on the stove to make herbal tea.

Puckett felt terrible for him. This was David's peaceful place. Now three armed FBI agents had broken that peace. Puckett watched him as he walked around his property. "I know this is difficult for you," she told him. "We don't want to intrude any more than necessary. We'll walk away and leave you alone here for as long as you like. When you're ready, come back to the car and we'll leave." She felt that Ted's arrest—if he was the Unabomber—would destroy the kind man now sipping tea in the desert.

A week after the trip to Texas, David phoned Puckett in San Francisco to ask if the FBI had eliminated Ted as a suspect.

"We're still working on it," she told him. And she promised, as always, to let David know if agents ruled out his brother as their suspect.

Puckett, aware the FBI had collected more evidence that pointed to Ted as the bomber, was almost certain the UTF would not eliminate him as a suspect. Agents had analyzed the postmarks on his letters, which showed no conflict with UNABOM attacks. This meant Ted could have mailed or delivered all the bombs. Agents also discovered that one of Ted's letters to David mentioned a story in *Scientific American*—a story also noted in the Unabomber manifesto.

The evidence against Ted Kaczynski was stacking up.

Three undercover FBI agents, all assigned to the UNA-BOM Task Force, flew into Helena, Montana, in late February 1996. They settled into the Park Plaza Hotel, a mile from the state capitol, in a historic section of town called Last Chance Gulch.

The agents soon briefed FBI Senior Resident Agent Tom McDaniel on their probe of Theodore J. Kaczynski. McDaniel was a burly lawman who wore cowboy hats, jeans, and Western boots. He had gained fame back in the 1980s for his role in dismantling The Order, a murderous gang of white supremacists.

People in small-town Montana keep an eye on outsiders, so the undercover agents about to slip into Lincoln

Ted Kaczynski lived in the woods near the tiny town of Lincoln, Montana.

to investigate Ted Kaczynski knew they couldn't dress like city slickers. As soon as Max Noel flew into Helena, he bought an extra pair of Wrangler jeans—along with thermal underwear and Danner hunting boots—so he could blend in.

The following morning, Noel and two of the agents drove up to Lincoln. The hour-long trek took them over snow-covered mountains, where the air was thirteen degrees below zero. They drove four miles south on Stemple Pass Road, once a stagecoach route. There, they spotted a cluster of mailboxes. One of them read TED KACZYNSKI. An agent snapped a photo.

The FBI needed to get a look at Kaczynski's cabin, but heavy snow was drooping the limbs of the towering trees, cloaking their view. They didn't dare drive up to his place, fearing their presence might spook him. They believed Kaczynski would hide or destroy evidence of his bombings if he got a whiff of the FBI's presence.

Noel and another agent popped into two hardware stores in Lincoln to see if they sold the same kind of one-inch avocado-green paneling nails that had killed Thomas Mosser. Neither store did.

The agents drove back to Helena and took seats at the bar of the Rialto, which sat across the street from the

The FBI shot photos of Kaczynski's cabin, which sat off a dirt road outside Lincoln, Montana.

local FBI office. They were joined by Agent McDaniel and a federal prosecutor named Bernie Hubley, a former FBI agent. They ordered a basket of popcorn and a round of draft beers.

"I know you're going to find this hard to believe, just as I do," Noel said to Hubley. "But we're here because the UNABOM Task Force thinks that one of your local residents . . . may be the Unabomber."

Hubley nearly fell off his barstool. He pledged to

keep the secret and help build a criminal case against the notorious Unabomber.

Noel and the other agents needed information only locals could provide. Agent McDaniel introduced Noel to Jerry Burns, a U.S. Forest Service law enforcement officer. Burns, who grew up in Lincoln and still lived there, patrolled the Helena National Forest. He seemed to know every citizen in Lincoln by sight, including the town hermit: Ted Kaczynski.

In the days that followed, Burns arranged to put two FBI agents on snowmobiles. He guided them to a ridge near Kaczynski's cabin, where they parked their rides. They crawled down a snowy hillside and crept to a spot about two hundred yards from their target's cabin. They had hoped to shoot a photo of the ten-by-twelve-foot dwelling, but it was hidden behind a wall of snow-covered pines.

Just then, the agents heard a door creak open and then slam. They crept away as quietly as a gentle snow.

CHAPTER 16

In the middle of March 1996, David Kaczynski traveled to Chicago to help his seventy-eight-year-old mother move from their family home to upstate New York, where she would be closer to Linda and him.

David had not yet shared his suspicions about Ted with his mother, Wanda Kaczynski. His mom was a proud woman who loved both of her sons. He dreaded telling her he had gone to the FBI, worrying that she might lose respect for him—or even quit loving him. He believed the news just might shatter what was left of his family.

At about this time, Freeman phoned Puckett. He wanted her to contact David Kaczynski and persuade him to write a letter to Ted. But Puckett balked. She reminded her boss that the FBI had promised not to use their informant that way. Freeman, angry that she wasn't following his order, chewed her out with some salty language. But Puckett held her ground. She reminded Freeman that she had promised David—on behalf of the FBI—that the bureau would not make him part of the operation. And she honored that agreement.

After David helped his mother settle into her new home, he phoned Puckett to tell her Wanda Kaczynski had a chest full of Ted's things. David knew the FBI would want to look at them, but first he had to prepare his mom for their visit.

On March 22, 1996, Puckett, Turchie, and Stark flew to upstate New York in hopes of interviewing Wanda Kaczynski. Molly Flynn drove up from D.C. to join them. After they all arrived, Puckett phoned David to let him know they were in town. Once again, he asked if the FBI considered Ted a suspect.

"We haven't eliminated Ted," she told him.

Some of Puckett's colleagues still believed Ted Kaczynski wasn't the Unabomber. Agents in Chicago had ridiculed her when she briefed them on her suspect. Even Agents Flynn and Stark, who had seen similarities between the writing of Kaczynski and the Unabomber, were not convinced he was the bomber. But Puckett, who had spent countless hours absorbing the words of the Unabomber and Ted Kaczynski, was convinced they were one and the same.

The following day, Puckett, Stark, Turchie, and Flynn parked near Wanda's new apartment in the village of Scotia, New York. Puckett phoned Bisceglie and reached him on a ski trip in Vermont. She asked if David Kaczynski had broken the news about Ted to his mother.

He had.

Moments earlier, David had told Wanda Kaczynski that he had some troubling news to discuss with her. He asked if she had ever read any news stories about the Unabomber, and she said she knew a little about the case. He brought up Ted's fixation with technology. Then, with tears in his eyes, he got to the point.

"Mom," he said, looking at his tiny mother in her big easy chair. "I'm really concerned that Ted might be involved with these bombings. I'm really scared."

Wanda's first reaction was to blurt out that he should not tell anyone. Then David explained he had already gone to the FBI, which was now investigating Ted. Wanda, stunned, said nothing for a moment. She climbed out of her chair and walked to David, who was more than a foot taller. She put her arms around his neck, pulled him down, and kissed his cheek.

"David," she said, "I know you love Ted. I know you wouldn't have done this unless you felt you had to."

A short time later, David answered the door at his mother's home looking miserable. There were still tears in his eyes as he introduced Puckett, Stark, and Flynn to his mom. Wanda told the agents she didn't believe Ted had committed any crimes. Still, she invited them to take seats in her living room, where she served them tea.

Puckett sat close to Wanda. She explained that the FBI had questions about Ted. They wanted to know about his early life, his hobbies, his friends, what he read. They also wanted to look at any letters he had written to her.

"I understand," Wanda said. "Ted has always been very different and alone. He lives in the wilderness because he likes it there. I think it suits his personality and lifestyle. He's never needed much in the way of money because he grows all his own vegetables and hunts animals for meat."

Wanda gave the agents permission to look through an old footlocker, which held a trove of Ted's letters.

Agents found a copy of the twenty-three-page essay that David had passed to the FBI. They also found canceled checks that showed Wanda had sent $14,000 to Ted in Montana.

Agents learned that David had also sent money to his brother. He had mailed $1,000 before the 1994 bombing that killed Thomas Mosser, and $2,000 more in advance of the 1995 Gilbert Murray bombing. David was horrified to think that the money he had sent Ted might have helped him buy bomb parts or travel out of state to mail deadly explosives.

Among the keepsakes Wanda shared with the FBI was a story Ted wrote in his youth: "How I Blew Up Harold Snilly." The tale included a list of ingredients in the main character's chemistry set.

"People like my son Ted are vulnerable to suspicion," Wanda said. She explained that her older son was an environmentalist who liked his privacy and condemned technology. But she could not say for certain Ted wasn't the bomber. "If it is him who is doing these terrible things, he must be stopped."

Agents later studied the letters they took from Wanda's home. They saw new echoes of the bomber's words. One handwritten note from Ted to his mother used the phrase "We can't eat our cake and have it, too." That was an odd inversion of the old proverb "You can't have your cake and eat it, too." Agents had only seen the odd version in one other text.

The Unabomber manifesto.

CHAPTER 17

The criminal investigation of Ted Kaczynski was such a closely guarded secret that many agents assigned to the UNABOM Task Force weren't aware of it. Secrecy was crucial. If word leaked out that the FBI was poking around in Lincoln, Montana, their suspect could flee to Canada. Worse, agents worried, Kaczynski might load his guns for a shootout with the FBI—the scenario that so worried David Kaczynski.

Agents were desperate to get a look at Kaczynski's property. But they couldn't tromp around near the cabin without being noticed by their suspect. So Noel came up with a plan. He made friends with Butch Gehring, whose home sat just up the road from Kaczynski's cabin. Noel confided in Gehring that the FBI suspected Kaczynski of mailing threatening letters and swore him to secrecy. What he didn't tell Gehring was that his next-door neighbor just might be the Unabomber.

Gehring, eager to help, led Noel and Burns, the Forest Service officer, on a walk toward Kaczynski's place. They were closing in when Gehring's dog spotted a deer and tore past the cabin barking his head off. Just then, the cabin door opened and a scrawny man with wild hair glared at them.

"Hi, Teddy!" Gehring shouted.

Kaczynski nodded, then shut the door.

Noel thought to himself, *My God, is that what we've been looking for?*

By the middle of March 1996, only Noel and four other agents were working the UNABOM case in western Montana. Their job was to collect more evidence in hopes that a judge would approve the FBI's plans to arrest Kaczynski. They also had to make sure their suspect never left Lincoln. The team uncovered hotel records and bank statements in Kaczynski's name. They checked library records to see what books he had taken out. They also checked bus schedules, learning that only two buses a day passed through town. Agents showed Kaczynski's photo to drivers on those routes, who recognized him

FBI agents stopped to shoot a photo of Kaczynski's mailbox as they began their investigation of the Unabomber in Lincoln, Montana.

as an occasional passenger. But the FBI uncovered nothing that proved Kaczynski was, for certain, the Unabomber.

About that time, Turchie showed Noel copies of Kaczynski's letters to his mom and younger brother. For the first time, Noel began to believe Kaczynski might be their bomber. Still, he wanted hard evidence, not just a lot of typewritten notes. He wanted what all the agents wanted—that Smith Corona typewriter.

The FBI needed an aerial photo of Kaczynski's cabin so agents could make a plan to surround the property.

There was no such thing as Google Earth back then, so an agent with a Nikon camera hopped in a small plane and flew over the place. He snapped an image so clear that Noel could see the cabin, the unpaved road outside, and the nearby forest trails. Noel knew the photo would come in handy when it came time for agents to move into position around the cabin.

In late March, the FBI dispatched more agents to western Montana. Agents began to worry that Kaczynski might get word about the sudden buildup. But on March 25, the UTF got some welcome news. The FBI had dispatched swarms of agents to the town of Jordan, Montana, about three hundred miles from Lincoln. There, a heavily armed antigovernment group called the Montana Freemen occupied a compound they called "Justus Township." Folks in and around Lincoln figured that the federal agents gathering in western Montana were on standby for the mess out in Jordan.

The next day, the UTF faced a new hurdle. Lowell Bergman, the executive producer for CBS's *60 Minutes*, phoned the FBI spokesman in San Francisco. Bergman said his sources had confirmed that the bureau was hot on the trail of the Unabomber and had sent agents to a state somewhere in the West to prepare for his capture.

The FBI shot this photo of Kaczynski's cabin when an agent aboard a small plane leaned out the window with a telephoto lens.

This was bad news for the FBI. Members of the UTF feared that CBS would broadcast a story before they could search Kaczynski's cabin. Agents knew Kaczynski had no electricity, but they worried that he might own a battery-powered radio and hear news that the FBI was closing in on him.

On March 29, Freeman met with Bergman at the FBI office in San Francisco. Bergman told the special agent in charge that he knew the FBI was ready to arrest the

Unabomber. To his credit, Bergman said he didn't want to broadcast a story that would harm the investigation. On the other hand, he didn't want to be scooped by his competitors. Freeman played dumb about the doings in Montana, but inside he was hopping mad. Someone had blabbed about the operation in Lincoln, which could potentially ruin the FBI's chances of safely arresting Kaczynski.

Two days later, Bergman let the FBI know he was aware that agents were flying into Helena and Missoula to work on the case. He told the bureau spokesman in San Francisco that his network planned to break the story the following day on the *CBS Evening News*.

Freeman, aware other news outlets were closing in, huddled with his agents in Lincoln.

"Okay," he said, "the down and dirty of it is this: CBS News is going live on the Montana suspect story in the next twelve to twenty-four hours, and it looks like the major newspapers also have the story and are set to publish."

FBI officials were forced to pick up the pace. They began to move hundreds of FBI agents and support personnel into Lincoln. As soon as everyone was in place, Freeman would give the order to move in on Kaczynski's cabin.

As the clock ticked toward the CBS broadcast, FBI Director Louis Freeh placed a call to Andrew Heyward, the president of CBS News. Freeh asked Heyward to postpone the story for twenty-four hours in the interest of public safety. Heyward, who had been on the job just a few months, agreed to hold the story.

The FBI's original plan was to apprehend Kaczynski as he rode into Lincoln on his bicycle. Noel and other agents worried that trying to arrest him at his cabin might spark a shootout. But with reporters circling, they now had to move in. First, however, they would need legal permission to enter the dwelling. They would have to persuade a judge that they would find evidence of crimes on Kaczynski's property. If they did, the judge would sign a search warrant that would allow them to enter their suspect's cabin.

Every American—even a person suspected of murder—has the right to feel secure in their home. The law requires judges to approve searches of a suspect's property. Police have to submit evidence to them to get permission. They write a document known as a search warrant affidavit.

On April 3, 1996, Turchie and prosecutor Bernie Hubley worked on their affidavit until 4 A.M. They had no hard evidence that Kaczynski was the bomber. But they had Kaczynski's writing, which echoed—sometimes word for word—the Unabomber manifesto. Their search warrant affidavit was 267 pages long, the length of a novel.

At sunup, Hubley walked into the federal courthouse. There, he dropped the affidavit into the hands of U.S. District Judge Charles C. Lovell. The weight of the document told the judge that this wasn't going to be a light morning of reading.

At about 8 A.M., the judge summoned Turchie and Hubley into his office. Lovell was intrigued by the unusual evidence the FBI had collected against Kaczynski—evidence based on his own words. Puckett's behavioral profiling partner, Jim Fitzgerald, had documented 160 similarities between the Unabomber manifesto and Kaczynski's twenty-three-page essay. Both documents contained similar phrases and concepts. Both essays also spelled some words the way people do in Great Britain. For example, he wrote "analyse" instead of "analyze," as Americans spell it.

"These word comparisons and the language study are something I've never seen before," Lovell told them. "Collectively, with all the other information, they make a compelling argument for the search warrant."

At 9:10 A.M., the judge told Turchie and Hubley he had found ample evidence to grant a search of Kaczynski's cabin. After signing the warrant, the judge shot Turchie a flinty stare.

"Now if this *is* the Unabomber," he said, "you go arrest him!"

CHAPTER 18

Terry Turchie sped north toward Lincoln, the ink of the judge's signature still drying on his search warrant. A half hour up the road, he stopped at a phone booth. Turchie dialed Jim Freeman at the FBI's command post at 7 Up Ranch, a motel and supper club just east of Lincoln. He told his boss he had the search warrant, and Freeman signaled for all agents to move into position.

The UTF had brought an army to Lincoln, more than 120 agents. Some wore white camouflage to blend in with the snow. They now kept watch in the hills near Kaczynski's cabin. Waiting to move in were explosives experts and evidence techs. A military bomb disposal team stood ready to enter the cabin in case it held a live bomb.

When everyone was ready, Freeman gave Max Noel

the signal to move in. For Noel, this was personal. He had worked full-time for three years on the UNABOM case, missing family meals, working weekends, and taking minimal vacation time. During that time, he had also seen his wife, a cancer patient, through rounds of radiation and chemotherapy.

Noel knew the horrors caused by the scruffy man inside the cabin. He was also aware of the potential dangers awaiting them. Kaczynski was armed, and he was more than capable of booby-trapping the cabin with a suicide bomb.

Puckett, awaiting a call to join the team in Montana, worried that agents might have to use deadly force during their arrest. For many weeks, she had promised David Kaczynski that agents would do everything in their power to bring his brother out alive. But as the FBI readied to move in on the cabin, Puckett's bosses ordered her not to contact David.

"They were worried he'd somehow contact Ted," Puckett recalled.

At high noon, the arrest team—Agents Noel and McDaniel, along with Forest Service Officer Jerry Burns—moved out from Butch Gehring's place. The two FBI agents wore

Three men moved in to arrest Kaczynski. They were, from left, U.S. Forest Service Officer Jerry Burns and FBI Agents Tom McDaniel and Donald Max Noel. They were photographed outside the elk lodge where Kaczynski was detained for hours before they placed him under arrest.

jeans and boots. Burns was dressed in his green uniform. Their footfalls made soft crunches in the snow. When they were near enough to the cabin to be heard, Burns called out.

"Ted! Jerry Burns, U.S. Forest Service."

Silence.

The three men trudged another forty paces toward the cabin door.

"Ted! We're just here to look at your corner posts."

Silence.

Noel wondered if Kaczynski had made his way out of the cabin, somehow passing FBI teams dressed in white camouflage.

The air was cool and still. Burns and the agents eyed the cabin door, which suddenly swung partway open.

Kaczynski appeared in the opening. He was painfully skinny from eating only the rabbits and porcupines he hunted. His face was blackened with soot from too many days huddled near his potbellied stove. His dirty hair stuck out in mad directions.

Burns stood directly in front of Kaczynski. "Hi, Mr. Kaczynski, I'm Jerry Burns, U.S. Forest Service."

He explained that the two men with him were from the Colorado Mining Company, which was leasing exploration rights in the area.

Kaczynski agreed to step outside. But suddenly he stopped and turned his head.

"I need to get my coat," he said.

He was whirling to go back inside when Burns shot both hands out, grabbed Kaczynski's skinny wrist and yanked him outside. Both men stumbled backward on the icy ground, struggling against each other. Just then,

McDaniel took a giant step forward and bent over, throwing his long arms around both men. He wrapped them up in a bear hug.

Noel pulled out his FBI credentials and a 9mm Sig Sauer pistol, which he pointed at Kaczynski's head.

"FBI!" Noel shouted. "We have a warrant for the search of this cabin."

Kaczynski quit struggling and glared at the man holding the gun, who now took a quiet, professional tone.

"I'm Agent Max Noel," he said.

Noel watched with quiet delight as Kaczynski's posture sank. The 170-IQ genius who had once described the FBI as a joke now saw that he was the punch line. After seventeen years, fourteen bombings, and the cruel murders of three people, it was over.

Ted Kaczynski had never seen the FBI coming.

Noel and his colleagues led their suspect to a nearby cabin used for elk hunting. They sat with him for five hours as agents and evidence techs picked through Kaczynski's cabin. His one-room dwelling had served as a bomb-making factory. The cabin's contents, as Noel later explained it, amounted to a confession of serial murder.

A few hours after Kaczynski was yanked out of his

cabin, Turchie made his way over to have a look inside. The FBI had strung yellow crime-scene tape around the dwelling, but the door was open. Turchie and Agent Pat Webb, the bomb expert who had raced to the scene of Gil Murray's murder in Sacramento nearly a year earlier, were standing on either side of the door looking at shelves choked with canisters of the chemicals that had fueled Kaczynski's bombs. Tears fell down Webb's cheeks.

"Terry, we got him," he said. "This is the Unabomber. We've solved this case."

In the late afternoon of April 4, Noel placed Kaczynski

Journalism students from the University of Montana captured the first images of the Unabomber after his arrest.

under arrest. Agent McDaniel shackled their prisoner with belly chains, and they hauled him back to the FBI office in Helena. Shortly after 11 P.M., agents booked Kaczynski into the Lewis and Clark County Jail.

Puckett, still in San Francisco, felt a little hurt to have been left behind. She had no interest in taking part in the arrest of Ted Kaczynski, but she wanted to be in Lincoln. She wanted to see Kaczynski's world for herself. A day or two later, Puckett's bosses in Montana sent word that they needed her. They wanted Puckett to evaluate the treasure trove of evidence that agents were hauling out of the cabin piece by piece. She flew in immediately.

The FBI's search of Kaczynski's place would take nine days. Agents discovered twenty-two thousand pages of essays, scholarly papers, and diaries that he had written during his sad, sick, solitary life. Among the papers were a packet marked "Autobiography," a carbon copy of his twenty-three-page essay, and the original Unabomber manifesto. Agents were thrilled to find the infamous Smith Corona typewriter he had used to type the manifesto. On the shelves of the cabin, they found coffee cans and other containers filled with bomb-making chemicals. They found many books, including a copy of the FBI fingerprint manual. (Kaczynski had eliminated his prints from the postage stamps by rubbing the paper adhesives with soybean oil and water.)

Puckett recalled standing just outside the cabin watching agents haul out a

FBI agents were relieved to find the Smith Corona manual typewriter that the Unabomber had used to type his manifesto, "Industrial Society and Its Future."

mountain of papers. She knew it would fall on her to read every word in preparation for Kaczynski's murder trial. She was overwhelmed by the realization that the UTF had finally caught the killer. She was also overwhelmed by the smell coming from the cabin. Kaczynski's body odor saturated the place. Even worse, it smelled like an outhouse: Kaczynski had no toilet, just a hole in the floor.

Puckett had taken a lot of heat from colleagues because she dared to declare that the Unabomber could not stop bombing. But after the FBI cut a hole in the roof of the cabin and searched its interior, an investigator found a package under his filthy bed. The box was wrapped, unaddressed, ready for shipping. It held a powerful bomb.

For six months, Puckett studied all of Kaczynski's words. It seemed he never had a thought that he didn't put on paper. She was grateful that Kaczynski was such a pack rat: His own words solved many of the riddles that had long plagued investigators. One mystery—the meaning of those metal "FC" stamps—had baffled the FBI for decades. Thanks to Kaczynski's papers, they confirmed that the letters stood for "Freedom Club."

Puckett had helped to close that club. That knowledge brought her a small, pleasant rush of justice. The genius killer, who had tried to force the world to believe his vision of freedom, would never taste freedom again.

EPILOGUE

Kaczynski's booking photo.

Theodore Kaczynski pleaded guilty to all his crimes, including the murders of Mosser, Scrutton, and Murray, on January 22, 1998. Less than four months later, a federal judge in Sacramento sentenced Kaczynski to eight life terms in prison without the chance of parole.

Today he resides on "Bomber's Row" inside the government's most secure prison, the Supermax in Florence, Colorado. He is inmate No. 04475-046. Kaczynski is confined twenty-three hours a day to a cell smaller than his tiny Montana cabin. (Officials later moved the cabin to Washington, D.C., where it was put on display at the Newseum.) Kaczynski rests his head these days on a thin mattress atop a concrete slab. His food slides through a hole in the door of his cell. Sunlight comes to him through a long, slender window. But through it, he cannot see even a glimmer of the world beyond the prison.

"I am afraid that as the years go by that I may forget," Kaczynski told an interviewer in 1999. "I may begin to lose my memories of the mountains and the woods . . . and lose that sense of contact with wild nature."

David Kaczynski was angry to learn from the TV news, rather than the FBI, that agents had arrested his brother as the Unabomber. Someone inside the U.S. government had leaked his name to reporters, and they had swarmed David's home. *CBS Evening News* anchor Dan Rather reported to the world that the Unabomber's own brother had turned him in. A late-night TV comedian called David the "Una-snitch."

Kathy Puckett phoned David to apologize on behalf of the FBI, but he angrily hung up on her. He later forgave Puckett, and they remain friends to this day.

The prosecutor who secured Ted Kaczynski's conviction called David "a true American hero" for turning him in. After the hearing, David read a statement: "My mother and I wish to reiterate our deep sorrow and regret to the victims. . . . You will be in our hearts and thoughts forever."

The Department of Justice gave its $1 million reward in the UNABOM case to David and his wife, Linda Patrik. The couple offered some of that money to Ted Kaczynski's victims. David hoped the money might bring them a small measure of comfort.

David's book, *Every Last Tie: The Story of the Unabomber and His Family*, was published in 2016. He lives in Woodstock, New York, where he is an activist against the death penalty. He remains saddened that his brother won't speak to him.

His mother, Wanda Kaczynski, died in 2011.

Jim Freeman, **Terry Turchie**, and **Max Noel** co-authored a book in 2014, *Unabomber: How the FBI Broke Its Own Rules to Capture the Terrorist Ted Kaczynski*. Turchie and Noel, along with Kathy Puckett and three other agents, won the 1998 Attorney General's Award for Distinguished Service for their roles in bringing Theodore Kaczynski to justice.

Freeman retired from the FBI before Kaczynski's

conviction, taking a position as director of risk management for the San Francisco office of Charles Schwab & Co. Noel, who has an almost encyclopedic knowledge of the UNABOM case, helped secure the Unabomber's murder conviction. He retired from the FBI in 1999. Since then, he has lectured about the UNABOM case across the globe.

Turchie stayed on to help prosecutors convict Kaczynski. In 1998, FBI Director Louis Freeh put Turchie in charge of the task force that hunted down and captured lone-wolf terrorist Eric Rudolph, a killer known as the Olympic Park Bomber. Turchie later became the FBI's deputy assistant director for counterterrorism. He still thinks about the Unabomber. When asked what he might say to Kaczynski today, he offered these words: "Ted, ultimately you were dead wrong. You were the one who wasn't as smart as you thought you were—the FBI wasn't too stupid to find you."

Kathleen M. Puckett, PhD, retired from the FBI in 2001. That year, she produced a study for the FBI's Counterterrorism Division on lone-wolf terrorists. She later coauthored two books with Turchie: *Hunting the American Terrorist: The FBI's War on Homegrown Terror* and

Kathleen Puckett at her home near Yosemite National Park.

Homeland Insecurity: How Washington Politicians Have Made America Less Safe.

Today, Puckett lives near Yosemite National Park. She serves private companies and government agencies as a behavioral analyst, security consultant, and expert court witness.

AUTHOR'S NOTE

This is a true story, an inside account of the FBI's long hunt for one of America's most cunning killers.

I grew curious about the UNABOM case in April 1996, when I covered Ted Kaczynski's first court appearance in Helena, Montana, for *The Oregonian* newspaper. I sat right behind Kaczynski in the courtroom, taking notes about the strange scene. I had met quite a few killers in my career, but Kaczynski didn't look or sound like any of them. I kept staring at this skinny, timid, soft-voiced man in the bright-orange jumpsuit. He was utterly confused when a gavel banged the court to order and a voice intoned, "All rise!" His lawyer had to nudge him to his feet, Kaczynski whispering, "Oh, I'm sorry." I kept thinking, *Could this really be the Unabomber? Did the FBI get the right guy?* The answers to those questions, as we would all learn, were yes and yes.

The Unabomber investigation had so many heroes

that I scarcely knew where to begin my research. When I discovered a 2008 interview of Kathy Puckett online, I could see she was a bigger-than-life character. I knew her vital role in the case would make a powerful story.

First, I had to go back to the beginning of the bombings, long before Kathy joined the UTF. I dove into the historic record, reading a thick stack of court papers, news stories, and interviews with key figures on the UNABOM Task Force. I read six books on the case, which provided amazing details and a lot of the dialogue in this book.

I wrote pages and pages of questions for Kathy Puckett, Max Noel, and Terry Turchie. I interviewed Kathy by phone, then spent two days interviewing her at her home in California. I spent a full day interviewing Max when he came to my town—Portland, Oregon—to address the FBI Citizens Academy. Terry answered written questions, followed by a phone interview. All three former agents answered countless questions by email.

Then I had to organize this mountain of information. I began by writing a long timeline of the life and crimes of Ted Kaczynski and the doings of the UNABOM Task Force. This chronology, typed into a Microsoft Excel spreadsheet, spanned more than twenty years. It began with the first bombing in 1978 and ended with Kaczynski's conviction in 1998. My timeline served as the backbone of this book.

I set several goals for myself as I began to write. I wanted to show readers the fear that gripped America during Ted Kaczynski's rampage from 1978 to his arrest in 1996. I wanted to introduce my readers to the agents who hunted him down. I wanted to put them in the middle of crime scenes and FBI bullpens and into the field with the agents who built this monumental case from San Francisco to Washington, D.C. Most of all, I wanted to show readers how a group of tireless agents finally, almost miraculously, brought the Unabomber to justice.

I hope you found this story as gripping in the reading as I did in the research and writing.

Timeline of Bombings

May 26, 1978, Evanston, Illinois

Terry Marker, a Northwestern University security officer, suffers minor cuts and burns while opening a package bomb delivered to Professor Buckley Crist Jr.

May 19, 1979, Evanston, Illinois

John Harris, a Northwestern University graduate student, suffers minor injuries while opening a mail bomb disguised as a cigar box.

November 15, 1979, over Northern Virginia

At least a dozen people suffer from smoke inhalation when a mail bomb explodes in the cargo hold of

American Airlines Flight 444. Smoke fills the Boeing 727's cabin, forcing pilots to make an emergency landing at Dulles International Airport, twenty-six miles west of downtown Washington.

June 10, 1980, Lake Forest, Illinois

Percy A. Wood, president of United Airlines, suffers cuts and bruises while opening a bomb hidden inside a hollowed-out book, *Ice Brothers*.

October 8, 1981, Salt Lake City, Utah

Students in the Business Classroom Building of the University of Utah discover a suspicious package in a hallway. Campus police call in army explosives technicians. They put the device through a portable X-ray machine and confirm that it holds a bomb. They move the device to a nearby bathroom and blow it up.

May 5, 1982, Nashville, Tennessee

Janet Smith, a secretary at Vanderbilt University, suffers serious injuries to her hands when she opens a mail bomb. The package was addressed to the head of the school's computer science department.

July 2, 1982, Berkeley, California

Diogenes Angelakos, a professor of electrical engineering at the University of California, is temporarily blinded while opening a bomb disguised as an electronic gizmo. The device, left in Cory Hall, causes serious injuries to his right hand.

May 15, 1985, Berkeley, California

John E. Hauser, a University of California graduate student, loses four fingers from his right hand when he opens a bomb left in Cory Hall. His injuries end his chances of becoming an astronaut.

June 13, 1985, Auburn, Washington

A supervisor at the Boeing Company opens a package and finds a wooden box inside. He chisels a hole in the container, exposing a metal pipe and electrical wires. Alarmed, he summons the King County Sheriff's Office, which dispatches a bomb squad to render the device safe.

November 15, 1985, Ann Arbor, Michigan

Nicklaus Suino, a University of Michigan graduate student, opens a mail bomb at the home of psychology professor James V. McConnell. The explosion leaves Suino with burns and fragmentation wounds. McConnell suffers temporary hearing loss.

December 11, 1985, Sacramento, California

Hugh Scrutton picks up a bomb disguised as a road hazard in the parking lot of his computer store. The blast is so powerful that it opens a hole in his chest, exposing his heart. Emergency rescuers put him in an ambulance, but he dies on the way to the hospital.

February 20, 1987, Salt Lake City, Utah

Gary Wright lifts a bomb off the parking lot of the computer store where he works. A massive explosion shoots debris into his face and upper body, severing a nerve in his arm, but he survives.

June 22, 1993, Tiburon, California

Charles Epstein, a geneticist at the University of California, San Francisco, opens a mail bomb in his home, blowing off three fingers, breaking one of his arms, and severely damaging his eardrums.

June 24, 1993, New Haven, Connecticut

David Gelernter, a Yale University computer scientist, opens a package that erupts in a deafening explosion in his office. The blast burns his body and fragments of the explosive mangle his right hand. He also suffers damage to one eye.

December 10, 1994, North Caldwell, New Jersey

Thomas Mosser, an advertising executive, is killed while opening a mail bomb in the kitchen of his home. His wife and young daughter, in the next room, are not injured. He is the second person to die in a Unabomber attack.

April 24, 1995, Sacramento, California

Gilbert Murray, president of the California Forest Association, takes a mysterious package to his office to open it away from his co-workers. The package bomb detonates on his desk, shooting pieces of furniture sixty feet across the office. Murray dies instantly.

The FBI had to cut a hole in the roof of Kaczynski's cabin to enter the dwelling, which held a store-house of bomb-making materials.

This is the only door to Kaczynski's cabin, which sat on remote land outside the tiny town of Lincoln, Montana.

FBI officials discovered a live bomb under Kaczynski's bed after agents arrested him. The cabin was a treasure trove of evidence. Kaczynski used his rifles to shoot animals for food.

Investigators believe that Kaczynski built bombs on the workbench inside his cabin.

The potbellied stove in Kaczynski's cabin kept him warm during long, cold nights in the frozen mountains of western Montana.

THE UNABOM CASE
BY THE NUMBERS

17 years, 11 months, 1 week

The time between the first bombing and the arrest
of the Unabomber.

$1 million

Reward money offered by the FBI for information
leading to the capture of the Unabomber.

53,000

The number of phone calls received at the FBI's
1-800-701-BOMB tip line.

2,417

The number of suspects identified by the UNABOM
Task Force.

11,800,000

Pieces of paper loaded into the UNABOM
Task Force database.

5,000 pounds

The weight of government legal papers turned
over to the Unabomber's defense team.

22,000

The number of pages—letters and other papers—seized
from the Unabomber's cabin.

170

The Unabomber's genius IQ score.

A LESSON IN PERSISTENCE

Agents on the hunt for the Unabomber took few days off. But one day in the summer of 1994, Terry Turchie stole a morning away from the case. He took his ten-year-old son Kevin to a baseball field in the San Francisco suburbs. They had just unloaded their gear when Kevin spied a man jogging around the outfield.

"Dad, that's Dennis Eckersley!"

Eckersley was the famous relief pitcher for the Oakland Athletics. Kevin, starstruck, could not believe his eyes. He begged his dad to drive them home to retrieve a baseball for his hero to sign. But Turchie told his boy that Eckersley probably didn't want to be disturbed during his workout.

Kevin simply would not be deterred. Paying no attention to his father, he hurriedly packed their gear into the car, and Turchie gave in. On the way home, he told his son not to get his hopes up. His hero, he explained, would most likely be gone by the time they returned.

Kevin Turchie met his hero—future Hall of Fame baseball player Dennis Eckersley—when his dad took a morning off to spend time with his son.

Sure enough, when they got back, Eckersley wasn't there.

Then, suddenly, there he was jogging into view. Kevin sprinted for an opening in the center-field fence. When Eckersley caught sight of the boy, he motioned him over and knelt in the grass. He signed Kevin's ball, bat, baseball card, and other memorabilia. There were no reporters around to see the baseball star's private act of kindness—just a beaming little boy.

"My young son's persistence and faith was an inspiration to me," Turchie would write years later in *Hunting the American Terrorist*. "And the whole event was a fresh reminder that, despite all the evil we had been chasing, there was good in the world. My batteries recharged, I went back to work."

WHAT IS A DOMESTIC TERRORIST?

Terrorists use violence, or threats of violence, to push their beliefs on others. The FBI's primary mission is to protect the United States from all terrorist attacks.

Many agents focus on domestic terrorism—attacks on Americans in the homeland. Terrorists on U.S. soil often hold extreme religious beliefs. These include white-supremacist groups such as The Order, which murdered people of color and Jews in the name of Christianity. Members of the Jewish Defense League have targeted Muslims and white-power groups for the sake of Judaism. U.S. citizens also have attacked their fellow Americans, claiming the authority of the Muslim terrorist groups al Qaeda and ISIS.

Other domestic terrorist groups hold extreme political beliefs. The Weather Underground set off a series of bombs in the 1970s to protest the U.S. government and its war in Vietnam. The Earth Liberation Front and its cousins in the Animal Liberation Front firebombed companies and government agencies they accused of harming the natural world.

No matter what terrorists believe, FBI agents and analysts work night and day to stop them from harming Americans.

ACKNOWLEDGMENTS

I am indebted to Kathy Puckett for her help with this book. She answered my questions with patience, grace, and good humor as I researched her remarkable story. I also wish

Donald Max Noel, at left, graciously answered many questions posed by the author, Bryan Denson.

to thank two legendary FBI agents, Terry Turchie and Max Noel, for sharing their insights about the long, difficult hunt for the Unabomber.

Many thanks go to my agent, Tamar Rydzinski, at the Laura Dail Literary Agency, who wisely conceived of the idea for the FBI Files book series.

Thanks to Katherine Jacobs, my editor at Roaring Brook Press, for her vision and expert handling of the words on these pages.

Many thanks to my friend and former colleague Bruce Ely for sharing a historic photo of Ted Kaczynski shortly after his arrest. Thanks to my friend and poker buddy Claude Laviano for shooting the photo of Max Noel outside the FBI's Portland field office.

I would also like to thank my young test readers, who carefully read a draft of this book and offered insightful critiques: Julia Druker, Claire Druker, Sophia Halpern, and Ella Halpern.

And a special thanks to Chris Allen, in the FBI's Office of Public Affairs, for his help and encouragement as I researched this book and others in this series.

Sources

Books

Chase, Alston. *A Mind for Murder: The Education of the Unabomber and the Origins of Modern Terrorism.* New York: W. W. Norton, 2004.

Freeh, Louis J., and Howard Means. *My FBI: Bringing Down the Mafia, Investigating Bill Clinton, and Fighting the War on Terror.* New York: St. Martin's Griffin, 2006.

Freeman, Jim, Terry D. Turchie, and Donald Max Noel. *Unabomber: How the FBI Broke Its Own Rules to Capture the Terrorist Ted Kaczynski.* Palisades, NY: History Publishing, 2014.

Graysmith, Robert. *Unabomber: A Desire to Kill.* Washington, DC: Regnery, 1997.

Kaczynski, David. *Every Last Tie: The Story of the Unabomber and His Family.* Durham, NC: Duke University Press, 2016.

Turchie, Terry D., and Kathleen M. Puckett. *Hunting the American Terrorist: The FBI's War on Homegrown Terror.* Palisades, NY: History Publishing, 2007.

Waits, Chris, and Dave Shors. *Unabomber: The Secret Life of Ted Kaczynski*. Helena, MT: *Helena Independent Record, Montana Magazine*, 1999.

Published Interviews

Freeman, Jim M. "Oral History Interview." By Brien R. Williams for the National Law Enforcement Museum's *Witness to History* program, September 19, 2014. nleomf.org/assets/pdfs/nlem/oral-histories -wth/Freeman_Jim_9_19_2014_updated_10_28_14 .pdf.

Noel, Donald M. "Interview with Former Special Agent of the FBI Donald M. Noel." By Brian Hollstein for the Society of Former Special Agents of the FBI, Inc., February 11, 2008. nleomf.org/assets/pdfs/nlem/oral -histories/FBI_Noel_interview.pdf.

Puckett, Kathleen M. "Interview of Former Special Agent of the FBI Kathleen M. Puckett, Ph.D." By Susan Wynkoop for the Society of Former Special Agents of the FBI, Inc., October 8, 2008. nleomf.org /assets/pdfs/nlem/oral-histories/FBI_Puckett _interview.pdf.

News Articles

October 7, 1993: Labaton, Stephen. "Clue and $1 Million Reward in Case of the Serial Bomber." *The New York Times.*

December 12, 1994: Elliott, Stuart. "Bombing in New Jersey: The Victim; Executive Had Vaulted to No. 2 Post at Agency." *The New York Times.*

December 12, 1994: Levy, Clifford J. "Bombing in New Jersey: The Attack; F.B.I. Says Fatal Mail Blast Is Work of Serial Bomber." *The New York Times.*

December 18, 1994: Blumenthal, Ralph, and N. R. Kleinfield. "Death in the Mail—Tracking a Killer: A Special Report." *The New York Times.*

April 25, 1995: Morain, Dan, and Jenifer Warren. "Serial Bomber Blamed in Death in Sacramento." *Los Angeles Times.*

April 26, 1995: Noble, Kenneth B. "Bombing in Sacramento: The Investigation; Bomb Meant for Predecessor of Victim, Officials Say." *The New York Times.*

May 9, 1995: "Nobelist Got Threatening Letter Day of Fatal Bombing, FBI Says." *The Boston Globe.*

July 5, 1995: Paddock, Richard C. "Professor Responds in Open Letter to Unabomber's Ideas." *Los Angeles Times.*

June 29, 1995: Paddock, Richard, and Shawn Hubler. "Unabomber Threatens LAX Flights, Then Calls It a Prank." *Los Angeles Times*.

June 29, 1995: "Unabomber Letters." *San Francisco Chronicle*.

June 30, 1995: Boxall, Bettina, Rich Connell, and David Ferrell. "Unabomber Sends New Warnings." *Los Angeles Times*.

September 20, 1995: Glaberson, William. "Publication of Unabomber's Tract Draws Mixed Response." *The New York Times*.

April 5, 1996: Marx, Gary, and Andrew Martin. "Survivors See Little Sense Behind the Terror." *Chicago Tribune*.

April 5, 1996: Walsh, Edward. "Sale of Illinois House Led to Break in Probe." *The Washington Post*.

April 9, 1996: Clines, Francis X. "Delicate Act of Go-Between Behind the Unabom Arrest." *The New York Times*.

April 14, 1996: Lardner, George, and Lorraine Adams. "To Unabomb Victims, a Deeper Mystery." *The Washington Post*.

June 19, 1996: Claiborne, William. "Kaczynski Indicted as Unabomber." *The Washington Post*.

October 18, 1996: Sward, Susan, and Bill Wallace. "S.F. FBI Boss Quitting to Take Security Post." *San Francisco Chronicle.*

May 24, 1997: Taylor, Michael. "Kaczynski Lawyers Criticize FBI Over Search Warrant." *San Francisco Chronicle.*

June 11, 1997: "Diogenes Angelakos, 77, Scholar Who Was Target of Unabomber" (obituary). *The New York Times.*

November 6, 1997: Warren, Jenifer. "The Blast That Ended His Dreams." *Los Angeles Times.*

November 11, 1997: Glaberson, William. "Unabomber Sought Revenge, Papers Show." *The New York Times.*

January 22, 1998: Lefevre, Greg. "Kaczynski Pleads Guilty, Avoids Death Sentence." *CNN.com.*

April 29, 1998: "Excerpts From Unabomber's Journal." *The New York Times.*

April 29, 1998: Johnston, David. "In Unabomber's Own Words, A Chilling Account of Murder." *The New York Times.*

May 3, 1998: Braun, Bob. "Widow of Unabomber Victim Doesn't Want Horror 'Sanitized.'" Newhouse News Service, *The Seattle Times.*

May 4, 1998: "Kaczynski Gets Life, Says Government Lied." *CNN.com*.

August 10, 1998: Kaczynski, David. "Blood Bond." *People*.

August 21, 1998: Claiborne, William. "FBI Gives $1 Million Reward to the Unabomber's Brother." *The Washington Post*.

August 21, 1998: Fagan, Kevin. "FBI Gives $1 Million to Kaczynski Brother." *San Francisco Chronicle*.

March 14, 1999: Brooke, James. "New Portrait of Unabomber: Environmental Saboteur Around Montana Village for 20 Years." *The New York Times*.

June 1999: "Interview with Ted Kaczynski." *Earth First! Journal*.

July 15, 2001: Kovaleski, Serge F. "His Brother's Keeper." *The Washington Post*.

June 26, 2008: "Percy Addison Wood" (obituary). *Chicago Tribune*.

February 19, 2011: Maugh, Thomas H., II. "Dr. Charles Epstein Dies at 77; Geneticist Survived Attack by Unabomber." *Los Angeles Times*.

February 23, 2011: Fox, Margalit. "Charles Epstein, Leading Medical Geneticist Injured by Unabomber, Dies at 77." *The New York Times*.

September 16, 2011: "Wanda T. Kaczynski" (obituary). *Tributes.com*.

January 13, 2012: "Clifford 'Butch' Gehring Jr." (obituary). *Great Falls Tribune*.

November 6, 2014: Dowling, Robert M. "Was the Unabomber a Eugene O'Neill Fan?" *The Daily Beast*.

June 25, 2015: Sanchez, Ray, and Alexandra Field. "What's Life Like in Supermax Prison?" *CNN.com*.

January 28, 2016: Bailey, Holly. "The Unabomber's Not-So-Lonely Prison Life." *Yahoo News*.

April 2, 2016: Erickson, David. "Lincoln Residents Recall Arrest of Infamous Unabomber on 20th Anniversary." *Missoulian*.

August 22, 2017: Davies, Dave. "FBI Profiler Says Linguistic Work Was Pivotal in Capture of Unabomber." *NPR.org*.

Photo Credits

Page ix: Federal Bureau of Investigation (FBI), United States Department of Justice; **10:** Terry Turchie; **16:** Federal Bureau of Investigation (FBI), United States Department of Justice; **18:** Federal Bureau of Investigation (FBI), United States Department of Justice; **23:** Federal Bureau of Investigation (FBI), United States Department of Justice; **26:** Federal Bureau of Investigation (FBI), United States Department of Justice; **33:** Federal Bureau of Investigation (FBI), United States Department of Justice; **35:** Federal Bureau of Investigation (FBI), United States Department of Justice; **54:** Federal Bureau of Investigation (FBI); **75:** Terry Turchie; **79:** George Bergman, 1967 / University of California, Berkeley; **90:** Federal Bureau of Investigation (FBI), United States Department of Justice; **92:** Federal Bureau of Investigation (FBI), United States Department of Justice; **102:** Federal Bureau of Investigation (FBI), United States Department of Justice; **104:** Federal

Bureau of Investigation (FBI), United States Department of Justice; **111:** Federal Bureau of Investigation (FBI), United States Department of Justice; **114:** Bruce Ely, 1996; **116:** Federal Bureau of Investigation (FBI), United States Department of Justice; **118:** Federal Bureau of Investigation (FBI), United States Department of Justice; **122:** Bryan Denson; **132, top center:** Federal Bureau of Investigation (FBI), United States Department of Justice; **132, bottom right:** Federal Bureau of Investigation (FBI), United States Department of Justice; **132, bottom left:** Federal Bureau of Investigation (FBI), United States Department of Justice; **133, top:** Federal Bureau of Investigation (FBI), United States Department of Justice; **133, bottom:** Federal Bureau of Investigation (FBI), United States Department of Justice; **138:** Terry Turchie; **141:** Bryan Denson.

Index

studying papers, of
    Kaczynski, T., 117
today, 122
Turchie and, 6–7, 38–40,
    48, 75, 121–2
in UTF, 6–7, 12–13, 39–41,
    80
al Qaeda, x–xi

R

Reno, Janet, 29–30, 65–8
Ross, Dick, 3–4
Rudolph, Eric, 121

S

Sacramento, California,
    130–1
Salt Lake City, Utah, 128,
    130
San Francisco Chronicle,
    53–4
Scrutton, Hugh, 20–2, 130
search warrant, 106–8
September 11, 2001 (9/11),
    x–xi
serial bombers, 42–3
Smith, Janet, 128
spies, 34–5, 38–9
Stark, Lee, 80, 87–8, 95–6
Suino, Nicklaus, 129–30

Supermax prison, of
    Florence, Colorado,
    118–19

T

technology, 58–60
Tennessee, 17, 128
terrorists, domestic, x,
    139–40
Tiburon, California, 130
tip line, UTF, 31, 61, 70–1,
    135
Turchie, Terry, 4
in conviction, of
    Kaczynski, T., 121
Freeh and, 121
Freeman and, 45–6, 53–4,
    79
Homeland Insecurity by,
    121–2
Hubley and, 106–8
*Hunting the American
    Terrorist* by, 121–2, 138
on Kaczynski, T., 121
in Lincoln, Montana,
    109
on manifesto, of
    Unabomber, 61, 64, 74–5
Moss and, 73–5
Noel and, 47, 102